Lizzie Selina Eden

My Holiday in Austria

Lizzie Selina Eden

My Holiday in Austria

ISBN/EAN: 9783337310127

Printed in Europe, USA, Canada, Australia, Japan

Cover: Foto ©Andreas Hilbeck / pixelio.de

More available books at **www.hansebooks.com**

MY HOLIDAY

IN

AUSTRIA.

SALZBURG.

BY

LIZZIE SELINA EDEN,

AUTHOR OF
"A LADY'S GLIMPSE OF THE WAR IN BOHEMIA."

LONDON:
HURST AND BLACKETT, PUBLISHERS,
13 GREAT MARLBOROUGH STREET.
1869.

CONTENTS.

CHAPTER I.

Our Holiday—Cabmen and Roughs—A Moral Waterman—A Rat—Escape from unknown Peril—Voyage in Rhine Steamer No. 26—The Captain's Autobiography—From Cologne to Bingen—The Convent of Perpetual Prayer—Arrival at Salzburg 3

CHAPTER II.

Berchtesgaden—A French Traveller—Austrian Dislike to Mutton—Austrian Sheep—Amulets of Snails' Teeth—The Austrian Frau—German and Bohemian Servants—Visit to the Salt Mines—Miners' Costume—Subterranean Lake 23

CHAPTER III.

Walk to Königsee—German Names of Flowers—Butterflies—Row on the Lake—The Obersee—Boats on the Lake—Our French Friend in Scotland—Ischl—The Dachstein—Excursions—Hotel Kreutz—Neglect of Ventilation—Intolerable Nuisance—The Promenade . . . 47

CHAPTER IV.

Beggars in Ischl—Dance at the Casino—Hungarian Pride—The Court at Ischl—The Imperial Family—The Clergy and the New Laws—Imperial Favour to Hungary—Wild Flowers—Cheap Fruit 71

CHAPTER V.

Walk to the Rettenbach Muhle—Accident to a Russian Prince and his Son—A Love-story—Hallstadt—Deformed People and Idiots—Visit to Obertraun—Journey into Styria—The Einspanner—Alt-Aussee . . . 93

CHAPTER VI.

Ebensee—The Inn and the Water-mill—King and Queen of Hanover—The Salt-Works—Process of Manufacture—Condition of the Workmen—Herr von Prinzinger—Mummy Children—A Suggestion to Baron von Beust . 111

CHAPTER VII.

Floating down Timber—Destruction of a Village by Fire—Cooking Salmon—A Dance in the Inn—The Emperor as a Sportsman—Trout Preserve—The Landlady at the Krahe—Shooting Lodge at Offensee—Virginian Creeper and Tea-plant—An Imperial Huntsman . . 133

CHAPTER VIII.

Linz—Military Music—Austrian Uniform—Promotion in the Army—Petty Jealousies—Recruiting—Women employed as Labourers—Navigation of the Danube—Scenery on its Banks—Military Cadets—Kissing and Shaking Hands—Vienna 153

CHAPTER IX.

Brünn am Geberge—Signal for the Village Cows—Senseless Game—State of Religion—Pilgrimages to St. Maria Enzensdorf—Absurd Ceremonies—Abundance of Fruit—Improvements in Austrian Inns—Schnellsieder—Preparation of Coffee 177

CHAPTER X.

Street Scenes in Brünn—Hungarian Ox-Drivers—Cultivation of Maize—Country Inns—Herr and Frau von H——Employment of Dogs—Petersdorf—Beautiful Church—Sufferings of Petersdorf from War—Besieged by the Turks—Jacob Trinkgeld—Destruction of the Hospital Church 195

CHAPTER XI.

German Vineyards—The Trade in Grapes—Austrian Wines—Straw Wine—Growth of Maize—The Marquis of Carabbas—The Vintage—Romance and Reality—A Vintage Supper . . . 215

CHAPTER XII.

Day at Laxenburg—House of Correction for Women—Count Chorinsky and Julie Ebergenye—Institution for Deaconesses—Palace and Gardens—Castle of Franzensberg—Mödling—Castle of Liechtenstein—Church of St. Othmar 233

CHAPTER XIII.

Railway from Vienna to Linz—Views round Salzburg—Caves of the Untersberg—The Sleeping Warriors of Kaiser Karl—Gnomes—A Prophetic Tree—Strife in a Convent—Appearance and Costume of the Peasantry—Dialect of the District 253

CHAPTER XIV.

Post-office Routine—Stamps—Official Neglect—Progress of Austria—Mönchberg—Château of Aigen—The Gaisberg—Politeness of Soldiers—Fox-shooting--Preparations for Winter—Cold Nights—The Peasants at Home . 271

CHAPTER XV.

L'Homme Propose, Dieu Dispose—Salzburg under its Winter Aspect—Unexpected Death of a Kind Friend—End of the Soldier's Warfare—God's-Acre—Funeral of Lieutenant-Colonel Ritter von Ari 293

Chapter I.

OUR HOLIDAY—CABMEN AND ROUGHS—A MORAL WATERMAN—A RAT—ESCAPE FROM UNKNOWN PERIL—VOYAGE IN RHINE STEAMER NO. 26—THE CAPTAIN'S AUTOBIOGRAPHY—FROM COLOGNE TO BINGEN—THE CONVENT OF PERPETUAL PRAYER—ARRIVAL AT SALZBURG.

CHAPTER I.

MY holiday began on the hottest day of the very hot June of the year 1868. We (that is, myself and a German friend) arrived in London on the evening of the 27th, to find the atmosphere almost suffocating, and to feel thankful we were only in it for one night. Our adventures began, on leaving Cannon Street Station, by finding that the drivers of both of our cabs were rather the worse for the trying weather, having endeavoured to mitigate the heat by imbibing freely. However, the more sober of the two pioneered the way to Hermitage Wharf, of which the other declared he had no knowledge whatever.

We had no sooner arrived there than from a neighbouring alley appeared a dozen street ruffians of the most ragged and unwashed aspect, who all clamoured vociferously for the honour of conveying our luggage to the boat which was to take us on board the *Batavier*.

It was a horrid, cut-throat-looking place, and our tipsy drivers fully sympathised with us. However, we ascertained that this really was Hermitage Wharf; and having accepted the chaperonage of some of these roughs to the end of the alley, in order to convince myself that the *Batavier* was really lying in mid-stream, we ventured to trust our luggage and parcels into the hands of the unwashed; and having followed them along the dark alley and down a steep step-ladder, we entered a boat. Then began the clamour for payment. I asked how much they wished. They proposed eight shillings. I intimated to them that sixpence a-piece was about what I considered ample remuneration. Of course a long argument followed, and at last I admitted that one box of books was rather heavy (it weighed over two cwts.), and offered, as the night was particularly sultry, to give another threepence to each man. Accordingly, I presented them with the sum of three shillings, assuring them if I had to sit there all night they should have no more. At the same time I felt I would gladly have given anything to get away from such a set of ruffians. Luckily they were tired of my stinginess, and went off tolerably contented. The cunning old waterman then remarked,

"It was such a shame to allow such men about. What a set of rogues they were to try and impose on ladies!"—concluding his observations with a long moral lecture on the sin of such imposition.

In four minutes we were alongside the *Batavier;* and in two more, ourselves and our luggage were safe on board. It was now the turn of the moral waterman to make his demand and receive payment. When I asked, "And how much am I to pay you?" he replied, "Well, ma'am, *I would not impose on you or any lady for the world, so I will say six shillings!*"

I really felt furious, and told him nothing on earth would persuade me to give him so much, particularly after his high-toned address. Then followed another long altercation, which ended by his assuring me any officer on board the ship would tell me it was not too much. The old rogue, having looked round, had seen that none of the officers were on board. However, as there were some officers of Indiamen or merchant ships waiting to go down in the morning to Greenwich, I appealed to them. One of them very kindly inquired into the number of our boxes, &c., and then assured me three shillings was ample. "Leave it here, ma'am, and if the man won't take it, he must go without." I thanked the officer, wished him good night, and we went off to our cabin.

Surely something ought to be done, in a great city like London, to guard travellers against such annoyances. Foreigners (especially with heavy luggage) travel by these steamers *viâ* Rotterdam very often, and get so abominably imposed on. Surely a very little management would be necessary to make such arrangement that proper porters, with a reasonable tariff of charges, might be established.

Next morning early we steamed down to Blackwall, where we took our passengers on board; among them two young German ladies, who were to be our fellow-passengers to Mayence. We had a bright day for our voyage down the Thames, and there was nothing to break the monotony but the usual substantial heavy English dinner, which occupied some time in the middle of the day. At night it came on to blow rather fresh, and the sounds of woe and lamentation arose from many parts of the ship. I was awakened by a crash, occasioned by a lurch which sent the water-jug and bottle into collision.

In the morning I begged the stewardess to see what damage had been done. She found the water-bottle broken, and the water all over the place. She proceeded to put it all in order, but presently interrupted her proceedings by a piercing shriek, and a call for the steward, accompanied by the unexpected exclamation,

"A rat! a rat!"

To my surprise, the youngest of the German sisters went into fits of laughter, and begged that the "rat" might be given up to her. On examination, the cause of the stewardess's alarm proved to be the frisette of her chignon! which she had put into the drawer of the washing-stand for safety the night before.

We arrived, as is invariably the case, too late at Rotterdam to catch the Rhine boat on Monday morning. We had, therefore, to spend the day as best we could, walking over the park, and through the streets, which are pleasantly clean and neat—nearly as much intersected with canals as those of Venice.

Early next morning we went on board No. 26 Rhine steamer, a small, cranky boat, on her last voyage. We had not left Rotterdam long before a curious figure came up the gangway, a female with a most woful countenance, with a stuff dress, nearly burnt to rags, hanging on to her. We were obliged to ask how she came into such a condition, and she informed us that she had been a steerage passenger on board the *Batavier*, in which there was a woman with two children, in the same cabin with her—the woman having a spirit-lamp, to make some food warm for the children. A lurch of the steamer having upset the lighted spirits, the whole place was instantly in a blaze, and it was not without considerable difficulty that the fire was extinguished.

Her burnt dress was a convincing proof of the truth of her statement; and as the other woman was on board with us, the Captain demanded from her the bottle of spirits, and flung it overboard. While we congratulated ourselves on our escape from this unknown peril of Sunday night, we naturally reflected on the terrors of a fire on board ship, that most frightful of all disasters, which it might have been our misfortune to undergo.

We had a very uneventful day, steaming slowly through the flat, ugly country, only occasionally stopping at a picturesque town or village to take in a few country-people, or some soldiers on leave. Except ourselves, there were no first-class passengers on board, and we were so unsocial as to think this very pleasant. There was, indeed, something very soothing and pleasing in the perfect calm all around, broken only by the sound of the paddles, and the occasional cry from the shore of a heron disturbed by the wash of the steamer from its grave fishing business. On the approach of evening we came to Emmerich, where the steamer stayed all night.

The Custom-house officers came on board, and were very strict in their search; the reason of which the Captain explained by telling us that a great quantity of lace was smuggled into Prussia by the Rhine way. For the officers of the steamers these visits of the Douaniers must be a most tedious affair. About eleven the search was concluded, and the Prussian officers left. All the passengers retired to their berths, except one of my German friends and myself. As there was a splendid moon, and it was quite warm, we determined to stay much longer on deck. Being also rather hungry, we had some English potted meat, nice Dutch bread and butter, and a bottle of Rhine wine.

The Captain of the steamer returned soon after from escorting the Customhouse officials on shore, and we begged him to join us, and have a glass of wine. He was very pleasant, and talked with a refinement superior to his occupation. Happening to speak to him of the navigation of the Rhine, and of the many large rafts on it, he told us that, more than twenty years ago, he had himself been nothing but a common raftsman on the river, till, by degrees, he rose to command one. That time, he said, was the happiest period of his life, for he then had a wife, whom he loved dearly, and who was as good as she was beautiful. She was always with him on the raft, and they lived contentedly and happily on it. After twenty years married life, without one cloud to overshadow it, she died suddenly of cholera, and left him with one little child, only three years old. Henceforth his raft had no charm for him, and he became mate of a steamer, and afterwards captain. He ended by saying that though he spent every day upon the Rhine, and saw many rafts on his passages up and down the river, yet he never passed one without thinking of his beautiful lost wife, and wondering if any of the rafts contained people as happy as they once were in those bygone days. He would not take any more wine, but wishing us good night, he went away to his cabin, where he told us the picture of his wife always hung.

Next day we pursued our quiet lazy voyage, going up slowly against the stream, till we stopped for the night at Cologne. There was enough daylight left for us to wander about the beautiful Cathedral, admiring the splendid stained glass through the bright summer sunset, and returning on board to sleep.

The following day came the well-known picturesque part of the river between Cologne and Bingen. At Mayence we took leave of our pleasant Captain and his rickety little steamer. I also bid farewell to two of my German friends, who were going on to Frankfort, and who had helped me to pass the long journey most pleasantly. Fräulein S—— and I landed and proceeded to the railway station, where we left our luggage, and went into the town. It was too late, however, to see the Cathedral, or the Convent of Perpetual Prayer, which my friend was very anxious I should see; but on applying at the wicket, the nun who answered us said it was beyond the usual hour of admittance. We had, therefore, to be contented with hearing, in the distance, the far-away murmur of the perpetual prayer, which never ceases. As soon as one set of nuns terminate their prescribed devotions at the high altar, their place is taken by another, and so the prayers are continued day and night—for ever!

At Darmstadt I said good-bye with great regret to my last travelling companion, and went on alone to Munich, and from there to Salzburg. The latter part of the journey was charming. I had again fortunately met with a most agreeable companion, with whom I enjoyed the beautiful landscape, which was illuminated by a full moon, shining brightly over a broken, varied foreground of hills, woods, and valleys. In such circumstances the beautiful view of the distant mountains of the Salzkammergut put sleep out of the question. The time only passed too quickly till we arrived at Salzburg, where the Custom-house examination was very brief. The officers were most polite, all they did being to mark my boxes with hieroglyphics in white chalk, a duty which they accomplished with a courteous bow and "kiss your hand." I felt I was once more back again in dear Austria.

I was very glad to arrive at the Goldenes Schiff Hotel, and hurry upstairs. Though it was past one o'clock, I was obliged to waken up the friend I had come out to join, and insist on her getting up and hearing all my adventures.

The view from my windows next morning delighted me, looking upon the principal square, with a beautiful high marble fountain in the centre. The design was highly ornamental, consisting of rock-work, and of large sea-horses and dolphins, spouting high jets of water from their nostrils. The Cathedral was just in front, and on one side was the Royal Palace, where the Empress Caroline resides; while on the other were the post-office and other public buildings. Here also is the main guard, with Austrian Jäger on sentry. Behind the Cathedral rise precipitously the picturesque rocks surmounted by the old Castle.

I was also greatly delighted with my friend's room. On opening a door in it I discovered an inner window, which opened into the interior of a small chapel (St.

Martin's). It was, of course, high up above the gallery, facing the high altar, where the silver lamp was always burning. The Goldenes Schiff is a most comfortable hotel, and its terms are very reasonable. In fact, rooms and food are much cheaper than in most of the small towns; and it is no slight recommendation that both the landlady and her son—who are most attentive to their visitors—speak excellent English.

Chapter II.

BERCHTESGADEN—A FRENCH TRAVELLER—AUSTRIAN DISLIKE TO MUTTON—AUSTRIAN SHEEP—AMULETS OF SNAILS' TEETH—THE AUSTRIAN FRAU—GERMAN AND BOHEMIAN SERVANTS—VISIT TO THE SALT MINES—MINERS' COSTUME—SUBTERRANEAN LAKE.

CHAPTER II.

BEFORE we finally left Salzburg, we went over for a couple of days to the beautiful district of Berchtesgaden. This little bit of Bavaria, which just abuts into the middle of the Imperial preserves, is only about twelve miles from Salzburg. It abounds in game, which is strictly preserved. This must be an intense annoyance to that keen sportsman, the Emperor of Austria, some of whose best chamois and black-game shooting lies in the immediate proximity.

We went by diligence next morning at an unearthly hour—even before the first early service in the little chapel into which our rooms opened. The day was lovely, and the road very beautiful. Of course, the scenery was not seen to advantage from the interior of the lumbering old vehicle in which we were journeying. The first three miles ran through luxuriant meadows, nicely bordered with large apple, pear, and plum trees; and we had the beautiful high peaks of the chain of Salzburg Alps before us all the way. Presently we entered a thickly-wooded glen, with everything to make it perfect— rills, rocks, tiny lakes, and, above all, the lofty peaks of the Untersberg and Hohe-Göll. We passed through a custom-house, but the examination is only a nominal thing, as we had not even to alight. We had only to answer the polite inquiry whether we had anything to "declare."

As no one is questioned on honour, I should think a small trade might be very easily managed here with forbidden goods.

I was much amused during the drive by a Frenchman who occupied the *coupé*. As the window between that compartment and the body of the carriage had been left behind, either for coolness or economy, I could overhear all his conversation with an Austrian gentleman whom we picked up outside the town. This Frenchman could neither understand nor speak one word of any language except his own, though he had travelled alone over the greatest part of Europe, including Great Britain. He complained bitterly that in Scotland he had almost utterly failed in making himself understood, either by signs or in any other way; and not only from the strong disapproval he expressed by words, but also from his expressive gesticulations, I do not think the "land of brown heath and shaggy wood" will ever again be honoured by his presence.

This gentleman seemed, too, to have an unquenchable thirst for knowledge, and one question he asked the Austrian I had often regretted, since my last visit to Germany, it had never occurred to me to put to any one. The important question was—"Why you never saw any flocks of sheep in Austria, and why you rarely or never have mutton?" The reply was, that in the more southern parts, where there are large plains, you find great numbers of sheep, but that "mutton is never willingly eaten by the Germans."

Since that day I have improved my knowledge wonderfully of the domestic economy of Austria; and before the end of the autumn I fully sympathised with the Austrians in their dislike of mutton, feeling strongly inclined to agree with them that it is decidedly unwholesome!

Sometimes, during the season in summer, you have some excellent dark mountain mutton, which is quite equal to Welch or any that I have eaten. But late in the year, when visitors have left Salzburg, and delicacies are rare, it is different.

Contrary to the express orders of the master of the house, we sometimes contrived a small joint of mutton for dinner, for a treat to our English appetites; but when it came on the table and was cut, we used to look guiltily at each other as we tried to eat it, and pretend it was excellent, though the fact was we hid great pieces away, as in our schoolroom days, under potatoe skins or pieces of salad. Anything so rank, so stringy, so disgusting, I never ate. After trying it twice, we gave in, and had to adopt thankfully the Austrian view, that their insipid veal and perpetual beef are, after all, most wholesome, even for sick people or young children.

In the end of autumn, when all the grain was harvested, and all the hay cut that could possibly be mowed off the rich pastures, I saw a few flocks of sheep on them. The very sight of them was enough to indicate that the mutton must be bad. The sheep themselves appear to be aware of it, for they have a sneaking, dissatisfied look, and always keep in a crowd, trying to hide themselves. Except in very old pictures, and in engravings in Bibles centuries old, I never saw such animals, with long flapping ears that would have gained any rabbit a prize for lop-ears, long legs and arched backs, like New Forest pigs. Even in the bitter winter weather they have scarcely any pretence of wool on their backs, certainly not nearly as much as a month old lamb. About Salzburg these were the only sort of sheep I saw; but I was told that great efforts are being made to introduce a better breed. Large sums have been given for some from England; and with the wonderfully rich pastures and mountain fields that they have here, what a rich return their introduction may make to the country!

They complain now that English wool manufacturers are ruining the woollen goods of Austria, from the superior cheapness and quality of their productions. They would be surprised to know how few fleeces it takes in Scotland to make a dress of home-spun, while here a whole flock would scarcely afford wool enough to make one even in times of reduced crinoline, short skirt, and no gathers! Still there is so much in prejudice; and from their ignorance the lower orders and servants are wonderfully prejudiced.

There is one—only one—person in Salzburg who can extract the teeth of snails. These, worn round the neck of a baby while teething, are an invaluable safe-guard against convulsions. The gardener's wife said she knew that snails had teeth, for on a still day she would listen while they were feeding, and could hear them biting with their teeth; but though they will wear these amulets, and eat the original owner (snails properly cooked are excellent), yet you cannot persuade servants to eat mutton, not even excellent dark-coloured mountain mutton, almost as good as venison! In Salzburg, mutton is only twenty kreuzers a pound, which would be about fourpence a pound

English, as their weight is much heavier than ours. Even the servants won't eat it, but prefer the stringy beef of which soup has been made.

I think next to Baron von Beust, the person most to be admired, and least to be envied, in Germany, is an Englishwoman at the head of an Austrian household, who can really keep things tolerably together. The amount of prejudice and ignorance in the servants you have to combat; the dread of fresh air and free circulation; the saints' days on which they won't work, and the Sundays on which they will; the greasy cooking; the beloved heavy puddings; the wonderful joints of meat; the dreadful knives that won't cut, and the good beer that won't keep! All these things are enough to turn the brain of a refined, practical Englishwoman.

I am not now speaking of the higher classes or the nobility. They are free from the prejudices to which I allude, and are much more enlightened and liberal. From what I have seen of their domestic life, it in most respects quite resembles our own in England. Among the middle classes, however, these prejudices reign supreme. The wives of professional men, who in England would live most comfortably, with good, trustworthy servants, and in an elegant, pretty home, surrounded by the comforts and luxuries of life, and in the enjoyment of society, pass their mornings in a state of perfect slavery, in slovenly half dress, either in the kitchen, looking after the cooking and the rubbing of the floors, or in the nursery, seeing that the unfortunate baby is not left in a tub of water, or has not choked itself with sour semmel. And this morning occupation is not the supervision that any woman willingly undertakes; but really hard manual work, doing the labour of an inferior class of servants! The consequence is that no time is left for mental cultivation, or for keeping up the accomplishments acquired early in life.

In the afternoon, after dinner, coffee, and an hour's sleep, you sometimes see the Frau Doctorin or the Frau General on the esplanade, or at the bath rooms; but generally they are too tired or too much occupied even for this indulgence. Even if tolerably well-educated women thus sink down into the condition of the stigmatized German Frau, one ceases to wonder that there is such a gap here between the nobles and middle classes, as the everyday life makes society impossible to the latter. Of course there are many exceptions, and, I am glad to say, among my own friends, some very bright ones; but in any town in Germany you will find that the reverse is the rule with almost all the wives of the doctors, lawyers, retired officers, and professional men. Till the servants in Germany are improved, I do not see how this state of things is to be altered. Their great faults are extreme stupidity and utter carelessness in the discharge of their ordinary duties—a happy-go-lucky sort of way.

From what I have seen in this part of the country, the Bohemians make the best servants, as they are decidedly more active, clever, and intelligent. But in the other countries of Germany there is a prejudice against them, as they say they are such thieves. There is a traditional story of three beggars—a North-German, a Sláv, and a Bohemian, who, travelling in company together, entered a house in which they observed a beautiful watch lying on a table. Shortly after leaving the house, the North-German remarked,

"That was a beautiful watch."

"Yes," said the Sláv, "and we might have taken it."

"I have got it," triumphantly exclaimed the Bohemian.

After we had breakfasted, on our arrival at Berchtesgaden (for we had left Salzburg about five in the morning), we drove to the salt mines, about a mile out of the village. Tickets to view them are bought at the office of the salt works, when the necessary number of visitors are collected to form a party. Proceeding then to the robing-room, we take off our usual dress, and reappear in Bloomer costume—long white trousers, dark tunics, leather belts and aprons, and rather elaborately ornamented caps. There were six of us, all feeling horribly shy and awkward, and staring and giggling at each other. None of us had courage sufficient to be the first to descend the stairs and join the ten gentlemen below, who, their dress also having undergone a metamorphosis, had been changed—at least in appearance—into working miners. At last I suggested to some of the ladies who had husbands below that probably they would be tired of waiting, and so prevailed on them to be the first to descend.

I could not help feeling surprised to see how the dowdy, common-place-looking women, in their smart holiday finery, came out quite pretty and graceful in their

Bloomer costume. We need not have felt so shy about our descent, for the gentlemen below evidently felt just as awkward and as foolish in their miners' dress as we did in our unusual attire. The salt-men themselves were too well used to the metamorphosis even to look amused, and took little or no notice of us. In fact, it would be out of character with the dress of a salt works official ever to smile or look amused; for though very striking and handsome, it is extremely sombre and funereal-looking. It consists of dark trousers and waistcoat, with a tunic-coat of black cloth, lined with black velvet. On the arm is worked, in silver, a miner's hammer and pick; and they carry in their hands, on grand occasions, a baton of silver, with a pick at one end and a spike at the other. A lighted candle was given to each of us to carry, and we were then marshalled across the high road to the entrance of the mine.

We followed the guides a considerable distance through a long undergound passage, through doorways, and up and down numerous side galleries, till we came to a very black, dreary-looking subterranean lake, which filled a large cavern. It was lighted all round the edge with hundreds of candles, which showed its dimensions, and made it look more gloomy and depressing. We entered a flat-bottomed boat, and were rowed first to a small fountain, the dripping of whose waters was the only sound to be heard in this awful place. We were then rowed to the opposite side, where we were landed. A more dreary boating excursion I never made—not even when, tide necessitating,

I have had to go off in a small boat and heavy sea to the Ostend steamer.

I should have felt still more uncomfortable in my mind had I known at the moment that this lake, which I only looked on as a saucer of ink, was in reality a fearfully deep pit of brine, filled by fresh water springs from the mountains, and afterwards thoroughly impregnated with the salt from the sides and bottom. After some weeks the water is drawn off, and conveyed to the salt works by means of miles of wooden pipes.

From this lake we proceeded down more galleries, and through more downward sloping passages, until we came to a large empty pit, which we were told was exactly under that filled with water, while yet lower was a third. There are, indeed, many ranges of these pits in the mine, some full of brine, or just emptied, and others where they are working, which are not shown. We had to descend in a queer fashion, which convinced us of the utility of our Bloomer costume, of which I had hitherto been rather sceptical.

We had to seat ourselves on a steep inclined plain, about fifty feet long. Five or six of us were packed together, with the guide in front, and we glided down with ease and velocity, arriving almost without a jerk on *terra firma*. Here we were shown the slimy clay or mud, with a thick coating of which they daub the floor to render it watertight before the spring water is let in. We were requested to pick up any specimens of salt we chose. There was a great heap of refuse bits, the prettiest of which were salmon or sulphur-coloured.

It is a great mistake expecting to find everything inside the salt mines bright and sparkling; on the contrary, all is dark and dismal-looking. In some of the galleries, when we held our candle quite close to certain spots which the guide pointed out, we perceived a faint sparkle where a vein of salt had been cut through. But it is all so mixed with earth, that it is neither beautiful in hue, nor has it a pretty appearance.

There is a little miniature chapel in the mine, decorated with all the best pieces they have collected. In a mass they look very beautiful.

We were very glad to ascend a sort of ladder out of the empty pit, and still more so to seat ourselves on a most peculiar railway car, like a bench on wheels. In this we found ourselves gliding rapidly down the declivity, shooting past side galleries, and over points which were all in proper order, for otherwise we must have been dashed against the rocky sides of the tunnel. At last, O joyful sight! like a star in the distance shone the blessed light of day, and in a few moments more we stood like owls blinking and blinded in the warmth and sunshine. Accidents occur very rarely in these mines, as great precautions are taken. In one or two places I noticed the galleries were propped up with timbers, but elsewhere everything looked solid and substantial.

The poor Frenchman did not come with us. I daresay he had not yet awoke to the fact that there were salt mines near, as we had left him in the hotel, pursuing flying waiters with painful contortions and elaborate gymnastic signs. When we returned, he was at one of the windows, making a painfully pre-Raphaelite sketch (with a very hard pencil on highly glazed paper) of a cockney-looking temple in an avenue of Dutch-toy firs.

Chapter III.

WALK TO KÖNIGSEE—GERMAN NAMES OF FLOWERS—BUTTER-
FLIES—ROW ON THE LAKE——THE OBERSEE—BOATS ON
THE LAKE—OUR FRENCH FRIEND IN SCOTLAND—ISCHL—
THE DACHSTEIN—EXCURSIONS—HOTEL KREUTZ—NEGLECT
OF VENTILATION—INTOLERABLE NUISANCE—THE PRO-
MENADE.

CHAPTER III.

AFTER we had dined at the inn at Berchtesgaden, we hired a boy to carry our carpet-bags, and show us the way from thence to Königsee. The walk is a very pretty one, passing through fir-woods for about three miles, and ending at the lake, where there is a tidy little hotel, in which everything is extremely plain, but fresh and clean. The place, which is very quiet, is surrounded with beautiful scenery, where one could spend a summer's month most pleasantly. There are many excursions by boat and on foot, and everything to enhance the interest of a quiet country life. He who is fond of botany may wander in search of the most lovely wild-flowers; the entomologist will find a great variety of curious insects; and the geologist or mineralogist may collect a large mass of valuable specimens.

The first evening we were there, the wood cutters came down from the mountains, wearing in their Bavarian hats great bunches of the scarce and beautiful *Cypripedium Calceolus*—what we call "Lady's Slippers," but the Germans, "Mary's Shoe." The common names for some of their wild flowers are very pretty. Primroses are called "Heaven's keys;" the early blue hepatica, "Heaven's stars;" snowdrops are "snowbells;" pansies, "stepmothers,"—a name which is thus ingeniously explained. The large lowest petal, with a spur attached, is the step-mother; the two lowest green petals at the back of the blossom are her two children; and the three upper petals are her step-children. The two side petals are the chairs on which her children sit; but the three step-children have only the two upper petals as chairs between them. The lovely little deep blue gentian is degraded by the name of "cobbler's nails."

A little wood near our inn was quite perfumed by quantities of the small lilac—*Primula farinosa*. The butterflies, too, are most beautiful; and a very great variety may be seen fluttering about. There are many kinds of the Argus tribe, large and small, pale blue and dark brown, almost black. I observed one beautiful large white butterfly, spotted with black and scarlet, just out of the chrysalis. Its wings were heavy with the morning dew, as it crept off a leaf and settled on my hand. It would have been a rare prize for a collector. There were also several sorts of Fritillaria, the dark green, the silver-washed, and another small sort.

I always feel grateful, when I see a Fritillaria butterfly, that I did not live in the Dark Ages! One sort of Fritillaria was called "Glanvil," from a Lady Glanvil, who, in those times, was fond of the pursuit of natural history. Her relations, at her death, attempted to set aside her will, by the assertion that no one in her right senses would go in pursuit of butterflies. An enlightened barrister, however, convinced the judge and jury that her conduct proceeded only from a laudable desire to study the wonderful works of nature, and thus succeeded in establishing the validity of her will.

We took a boat one day from the end of the lake, about three miles. The shores were very winding and lonely, with splendid perpendicular mountains bluff down to the water's edge, which was fringed with beautiful woods of fir, on the border of which we perceived the scarlet rhododendron hirsutum (*rose des Alpes.*) Of course the boatman obliged us to land, and see the waterfall at Königsbach; but it is not worth the trouble. We firmly resisted being taken to the Bartolomäus See; and when the boatmen said they were hungry and wanted to eat, we told them we were also hungry, but wished to go to the end of the lake instead of eating. They laughed and rowed on. I think their hunger was imaginary. At the far end of the lake they shewed us some chamois scrambling about the loose rocks far above.

This place is famous for these elegant creatures, as it is strictly preserved for the Bavarian king, who never hunts.

We landed at the end, and walked across a bit of rough land to the small lake of Obersee, a charming spot, shut in by precipices on three sides. At the end the dark rocks are overlooked by beautiful mountain tops crowned with snow, from whence the Schrambach falls into the lake, which lies dark and gloomy in its nest. The only sounds we heard were those of the waterfalls, at the further end, faint and distant. Nearer, we heard the sound of small stones descending in a shower into the water, every now and then thrown down by some scrambling chamois, far up among the loose rocks on the side of the precipice. The only living thing besides was an eagle soaring high above our heads, no doubt wondering what we were doing in his domains. At our feet in the lake lay the bleaching skeleton of some deer or sheep. The scene altogether might be called "a savage but magnificent one."

We were quite sorry when our sketches were finished, and we had to leave it. We soon found our boatmen, who had forgotten their hunger in a comfortable and sound—or rather unsocial—sleep. The sound of our steps roused them. Mountaineers and poachers (one of our boatmen I had seen return home the day before with his gun and a full bag) sleep very lightly. We got into our boat and were rowed back.

These boats, which are cut out of the trunk of a tree, are detestable. They are very heavy and unsafe, the least movement upsetting them. The sides of the lake, by the numerous crosses erected on them, show how many accidents have terminated fatally. Primitive, however, as is the construction of these boats, if you can only banish from your mind all idea of danger, or forget their uncomfortable jerky motion, they are admirably adapted for seeing the scenery to the greatest advantage. The visitors sit near the bow, with their backs turned to the rowers, who, if there are two, take their place in the stern and propel the boat, one standing and one sitting. As they change places occasionally, one then trembles for dear life, for in appearance the boats are very unsteady.

We survived these perils, however, and in compassion of the hunger they had endured, gave the boatmen an extra trinkgeld. We found a soldier on furlough to carry our bags, and, walking through the pretty woods full of wild flowers, caught the diligence at Berchtesgaden, and returned to Salzburg. The Frenchman was our only travelling companion back; but this time we changed places, we being in the *coupé*, and he having the body of the carriage to himself.

Half way between Berchtesgaden and Salzburg, close to the Bavarian frontier, the two diligences meet and exchange horses. As they had so few passengers this day, we were turned out into the Salzburg diligence; but the Frenchman sat immovable in the interior, not understanding a word, and no doubt wondering what strange Custom-house regulations were in force here. My companion told him in a few words the state of the case, and he nimbly alighted. He was boundless in his expressions of gratitude, but we were left in wonder how such a traveller could possibly ever arrive safe at his destination.

Beyond the pleasure of seeing new scenes and foreign cities, there can be little enjoyment in travelling quite alone, especially when not understanding a word of the language. No wonder he found Scotland difficult to travel in! I can picture to myself the mincing polite Frenchman in the middle of a turf-smoked kitchen in the beautiful Highlands of dear Scotland, refusing those savoury national dishes, haggis and hotchpotch, and turning in disgust from whisky toddy. "Hout, mon! but ye're a dainty chiel."

What would he think of a Sunday in Edinburgh, the most dreary and desolate festival in the world? Truly he must have many gloomy recollections of that beautiful land, to brood moodily over, and to embitter his holiday remembrances. No doubt he often shakes his finger wrathfully at his crabbed little sketches of lofty Ben Lomond and rugged Schehallion.

From Salzburg we determined to post to Ischl, as we were told it was a road on which there was a great deal worthy of the traveller's observation. The drive takes about six hours, and is certainly very beautiful. We begin by ascending a very long hill (for which we have to take on two more horses), directly on leaving Salzburg, at a place that rejoices in the name of Gniggl. The ascent is not very steep in any part, but it is wearisomely long. At the top is a small lake, pretty, with hills all round. The place appeared to be a summer retreat from Salzburg, as there were many villas scattered about, which belonged to tradesmen of that city.

We dined at Hof, and for the first time had delicious mountain trout for dinner. Soon after leaving Hof, we saw the beautiful mountains round Ischl rising in the distance; and, after ascending a steep hill, again stopped to bait the horses and have some excellent Austrian coffee at the little inn at St. Gilgen.

After that it is a flat drive through pretty wooded country, by the side of the stream Ischl, till we arrive at the beautifully situated town of that name. Nature has done everything she possibly could for Ischl, there is nothing left to be wished for. Two beautiful rivers run through the town, clear and sparkling, of that wonderful deep green colour that so many mountain streams possess. Mountains, rugged, picturesque, and magnificent, environ the city. Lower down at their base are smaller hills, covered with fir woods and forest trees, which contrast agreeably with the pleasant emerald green patches and the rich pasture lands. There are short walks to glens of dark pines, even in the summer cool and refreshing, from the heavy over-spreading branches, not to speak of the mountain torrents that rush tossing and tumbling over rocky beds— sweeping swiftly past your very feet.

One may also climb a neighbouring hill, and after passing through pleasant Alpine pastures, come upon some small quiet lake, guarded round by iron-grey precipices, on the summits of which, and in deep dark nooks, the eternal snow, lying hidden from the sun, seems, by its cooling aspect, mockingly to allure the tired and heated pedestrian vainly trying to find a shelter from the blazing beams of the fierce July sun.

It requires very little exertion to walk far enough to obtain a sight, any clear day, of the Dachstein, with its fields of sea-green ice and snow, only warming into life when the setting sun tints its summit with that exquisite rose-blush by which snow and limestone mountains seem to rival the overhanging clouds in beauty and softness of hue.

For those who are not afraid of a long walk and a good climb, Ischl is first-rate head-quarters. In whatever direction one may set off, he is sure to find charming excursions of two or three days' duration, to mountains, lakes, or waterfalls. And it is not the least advantage that in these remote districts there are such clean and tidy little inns, at which he may sleep, and have a good supper of trout and potatoes, very often Schnitzel, and always good coffee. The black bread is rarely liked at first, but after a time one finds it extremely good, especially with fresh pasture butter. The Gemsfleisch (Chamois) is never worth eating, not even when shot by the Emperor, as they informed us one day at an hotel in Ischl, where we usually dined, a recommendation which, in their opinion, ought to have given it a peculiar relish. We generally dined at the Hotel Kreutz, the landlord of which is particularly civil and attentive, and where the cooking is extremmely good. It is far the best hotel in Ischl, and moderate in its charges, compared with the Hotel Bauer or the Kaiserin Elizabeth. The Hotel Bauer is most beautifully situated on the Calvariensberg, but the ascent to it is a most wearisome pilgrimage, after a hard day's walking, or in the heat of the sun.

It would be a great comfort for English travellers if they might have a little more fresh air in the table d'hôte rooms. Even in summer, with the thermometer as high as it can well go, there is sure to be some delicate child, or some person with a chest complaint, who cannot live with fresh air. The doctors in Austria are much more enlightened on the subject of ventilation than the people themselves; and most of them now recommend attention to its salutary rules. It is amazing, however, how unenlightened many even of the educated classes are on this all-important subject. Women may be constantly seen walking for hours on a promenade, with a low dress and short sleeves, only covering their arms and neck with the thinnest tulle.

Yet directly they come into a room they cannot bear a breath of air, and sit in a close, unhealthy atmosphere, which makes them white and sickly-looking; while the children are always delicate and half-grown. What indeed can be expected from people who in winter never open a window even for a few moments, to renew the air in their apartments; and, what is worse, directly the first bracing frost makes itself felt, cram every aperture in their houses, every crack and cranny, with moss, and live for five months of the year in the stifling fumes of an over-heated stove.

With regard to the table d'hôte, added to the horrible closeness of the room, where thirty or forty people are dining, is the perpetual smell of tobacco smoke, which is enough to make one loathe bad cigars for ever. It really ought to be insisted on that the hours for smoking, which are usually printed in large letters in most of the table d'hôte rooms, should be adhered to. Many people have a great dislike to tobacco smoke; and I for one should never get used to eating any meal with clouds of nicotian vapour floating around my head, and communicating its not very attractive flavour, and exceedingly disagreeable taste, to everything with which it comes in contact.

One day two Prussians were sitting at our table, smoking such strong tobacco, that we had to leave the room. Next day we asked the civil landlord to place us at a table where there was no smoking. He took us to one at which two gentlemen were sitting. "They are English," he said, "and I am sure will not smoke when ladies are dining." So we sat down and began our dinner contentedly. Presently began the "Englishmen"—

"How did you relish your chicken, General?"

"I calculate, Colonel, that our stiffish walk to-day banged any in our little campaign," &c., &c.

Americans abound in Ischl; but Jews more than any other nation. It is said that more than half the visitors are of Hebrew origin. From the "Guest Lists," unless the name of the nation follows that of the visitor, it is impossible to guess his country. Such wonderful mistakes are made with the names and qualifications of the visitors! For instance, we observed such entries as "Miss Brown and daughter;" the "Rev. General Smith," &c. My name was put down "Essen."

For those who think scenery a bore, there

is a pretty promenade by the side of the Traun, where, under the shelter of the trees, you can eat ices and drink coffee, or parade up and down in most elaborate toilettes, to the sound of a very second-rate band, and enjoy yourself quite as much as if you were in Vienna.

In the dust and chatter one quite forgets that he is in the midst of some of the most perfect of God's creations, untouched and unimpaired by those works which in other countries, where life is more stirring and active, are rendered necessary by the demands of manufacturing industrial, or commercial progress. I believe there were many people at Ischl who never went beyond the promenade; but morning, noon, and evening, sauntered up and down, displaying to the envious gaze of their fellow-loungers, dresses of lace and tulle only fit for a ball-room, or, if gentlemen, equally splendid uniforms, not to speak of thin boots with heels of surpassing height, or dress-shoes with enormous rosebuds.

Through this elegant crowd some dusty travel-stained Englishmen might occasionally be seen making their way, with that haughty and independent bearing which they so often assume among foreigners. They looked strong, sturdy, and manly, in their homespun or frieze suits, thick boots, and burnt hands and faces, as, carrying their knapsacks and fishing-rods, they went to, or returned from, their sport.

Chapter IV.

BEGGARS IN ISCHL—DANCE AT THE CASINO—HUNGARIAN PRIDE—THE COURT AT ISCHL—THE IMPERIAL FAMILY—THE CLERGY AND THE NEW LAWS—IMPERIAL FAVOUR TO HUNGARY—WILD FLOWERS—CHEAP FRUIT.

CHAPTER IV.

IN Ischl beggars abound. In the streets, at the doors of the hotels, at all the cafés and restaurants, you are sure to meet them. They knock at your sitting-room door, or find their way to your kitchen for broken food. They don't care, luckily, to go very far from the fashionable crowd, and the promenade is their favourite resort, though there are notices in every walk forbidding their entrance.

I have often been amused at their impudence. I have seen a regular old stager seated under a tree with a board over his head, inscribed not with the heart-melting appeal,

"Pity the poor blind," or, "I am starving," but the apparently peremptory police ordinance, "Begging is here strictly forbidden." It is no use informing them politely that you are not disposed to give, or that you have no small change; the only thing that has any effect on them is a quick decisive Austrian "Marsch."

They must make an excellent living during the season. Few people refuse to give them a kreuzer, and they are never too proud to accept this very small coin. The amount collected during the day, even in this insignificant coin, the value of which is so trifling that it has no equivalent in English money, must generally be a good sum. Besides money, they drive a very good trade in broken victuals. An acquaintance of mine, who had to visit professionally at a small inn of third-rate class, found one room filled with fragments of bread of all sorts. On inquiring what was the object of such a collection, he was told that this was a receiving-room for the scraps beggars brought in exchange for "schnaps." The people of the house, it appears, kept a great many pigs, which they fed entirely on this broken bread.

Every week at Ischl there was a public dance at the Casino (admittance fifty kreuzers!). This entertainment must have been very pleasant to the select few who kept exclusively together at the upper end of the room. Of course, there was a great mixture of classes in the *salle*, and every one went in bonnets or hats, which, as the ball began at eight, and ended at twelve, was rather absurd. This foreign custom, too, is dreadfully fatiguing. Directly you stop with your partner to rest in the valse or galop, any gentleman in the room may come up and ask you for a turn; so that, however fond of dancing a girl may be, it is extremely hard work. From my quiet corner of the room I noticed this unreasonable exaction, and pitied some of the young dancers of my own party, who declared they were half dead!

I was much amused watching one Hungarian gentleman of our acquaintance in the mazurka, a dance on which he particularly prided himself. We had for some time agreed he was dreadfully conceited, but this evening his self-estimation passed all bounds, as in his national dress, with his head thrown back and his eyes half closed, he performed a few steps languidly under the centre chandelier. Then, to all appearance suddenly awaking to a sense of what society required from such a splendid specimen of his glorious nation, he would whirl his partner breathlessly round, or dash frantically from one end of the room to the other.

I was told an anecdote illustrative of Hungarian pride. The incident occurred at a ball at Pressburg last winter. A young lady, who thought herself demeaned by having for a *vis-à-vis* a young officer who was not a noble, hardly allowed him to touch the tip of her little finger when she passed him in the quadrille. The second time, thinking even this slight favour too great a condescension, she held him the corner of her pocket-handkerchief! He coolly took it, used it, and returned it to her! Not a gentlemanly thing to do, but it served her quite right.

Ischl was much enlivened by the presence of the Court, but rumour says the

Empress was so disgusted with the insolent way that people stared at her—even through their opera-glasses—that she will never go there again. The little Prince Imperial was always out walking with an officer, his governor, no matter what the weather was; and in this, as in other nursery arrangements, the royal children are much better managed than most German families. They have an English nurse, and the little baby has a long white robe—not the dreadful mummy bandages in which most Austrian babies are packed and folded—a fearful remnant of barbarism, which, I believe, is now almost entirely confined to the peasants and lower orders; and it will be in the interests of humanity when it is abolished among them also.

We were walking one day in a wood two or three miles from Ischl, when, on the other side of the river, at a little distance, we saw one of the royal carriages, which stopped, and the little Prince and his governor alighted, the carriage being sent away. They had not gone many yards before they met a poor family who begged of them. A few words passed between the Prince and his governor, and the carriage was hailed. The footman came running back, and taking out his purse, handed some change to the poor people. There had been evidently a dearth of small money in the royal purse, but a good feeling was shown in thus taking the trouble to send for the money for the poor wanderers. It will be a great pity if it is true that the Court will not come again to Ischl; for when they were allowed to pass their time quietly, they seemed to enjoy themselves so much.

On the birthday of the little Princess Gisela, the Emperor came purposely from Vienna to spend it with his family, and they were seen during the day at a small "restauration" on the hills, taking coffee. Luckily there were very few people about, and they were able to enjoy themselves in the luxury of solitude. Another day, as we were walking in a retired part of the promenade, we met an officer with a lady leaning on his arm. If it had not been for the large wolf-hound that generally accompanies the Empress, we should not at first have recognized Her Majesty and the Emperor. She is extremely pretty, with a very bright, sweet smile, and a slight, graceful figure. She was always dressed with great taste, and this day wore a pale grey dress, hat, and boots, the two former trimmed with fringes of little mother-of-pearl Venetian shells.

Much more state was kept up by the father and mother of the Emperor, who lived next door to us, and never moved without attendants. Once only, during the visit of the King of Saxony, we met His Majesty and the Archduke walking perfectly unattended, and mixing unrecognized among the crowd, composed principally of foreigners. I never could look on the Archduchess without feeling a deep compassion and pity for the mother whose strong, ambitious disposition and ultramontane views had been so deeply engrafted in her beloved but unfortunate son, whose last words were, "Do not bind my eyes, or else I cannot see my mother's spirit." What the heart can bear, and not only overlive, but even learn to enjoy life and its pleasures once more! Only a year since the echo of the regicidical volley which carried death to the heart of the brave Emperor Maximilian excited a thrill of horror in every civilized land; and yet even in his father's Court you now look in vain for one outward sign of mourning for this beloved but unfortunate scion of the House of Hapsburg.

The genealogical relations of the Royal Family of Austria are a most bewildering problem to a foreigner, especially when one hears people talking casually of two Emperors and three Empresses, besides the poor Empress Charlotte, and the father and mother of the Kaiser. As far as *entourage* and Court show go, there are virtually three Emperors and five Empresses, besides a Royal Family of twenty-four Archdukes and Archduchesses!

The ex-Emperor Ferdinand, and his Empress, keep up a dreary ecclesiastical state in the beautiful old palace in the Hradschin at Prague. The Empress Caroline, widow of Kaiser Franz, lives at Salzburg. In 1867, however, she turned out to accommodate the Austrian and French Emperors, when they met there—a meeting of which the world talked so much, though eventually it proved to be little more than a friendly visit, in a convenient and most picturesque city. The poor widowed empress of Kaiser Max is never likely to return to the scene of her early days of happy married life; and the Archduke and Archduchess Franz Karl, the father and mother of Kaiser Franz Josef, live in different royal residences during the year.

Scarcely a large town in Austria has not an Imperial Palace; and certainly every city has one, if not two. Imperial hunting and shooting boxes abound wherever there is an eligible site to erect one! There is, indeed, no want of royal residences; and the incomes for so many crowned and uncrowned heads must be very considerable. The Emperor appears to be much liked, everyone concurring in the opinion that he is thoroughly goodhearted. He is inordinately fond, however, of sport and pleasure, and has all the prejudice which is so marked amongst the nobles in Austria in favour of high birth and of the priests. It must have cost him a hard struggle to sign the "Consessionellen Gesetze."

Already the clergy of Austria are rising up like a swarm of angry bees; and not only is their buzzing heard, but their stings are felt throughout the length and breadth of the land. There must for a time be a sharp struggle, and then things will calm down; but at present, in almost every city and town of Austria, meetings of the clergy are held. Those, however, who are enlightened and liberal, plead illness as an excuse for keeping away from these useless discussions; and those who feel hopeless and angry, denounce from their pulpit the wickedness of the new laws. They go, too, among their people, and working on the credulity of the women, tell them that the marriage ceremony must always be a sacrament. Congregations of these sympathetic beings leave the churches in tears, having been assured by the priests in their sermons that the civil law of marriage will not be binding, and that now men will have as many wives as they please! In future we shall no longer hear of those absurd barriers to marriages between Protestants and Roman Catholics; and the children of such mixed unions will be brought up in whatever religion the parents themselves choose. In short, Protestants will soon cease to be looked upon in Austria as the wicked heretics they have hitherto been considered; and as the simplicity and purity of their religion begins to be understood, it will be welcomed by a people to most of whom it has either been wilfully misrepresented, or shrouded in dark mystery, but in whose minds more advanced, liberal, and independent views are now beginning to dawn. The schools, too, are to be taken from the sole and exclusive supervision of the Roman Catholic priests, and to be placed under Government inspectors.

Thus Austria, which was the only country to sign the Concordat, has at length shaken it off; and it is a subject of much comment in all parts of Germany, that of the four great powers, France, Austria, Italy, and Spain, who were the chief supporters of the Papal sway, only the first remains true! Austria has broken the Concordat, Italy has again and again risen in arms against the Pope, and Spain, by throwing off the yoke of a bigoted Queen, has now inaugurated the era of its spiritual freedom.

Just now every one in Austria is jealous of the Hungarians, and doubly jealous of the favour shown them by the Emperor and Empress. The latter especially is supposed to have a strong leaning towards Hungary, and the most ridiculous stories are afloat relative to her dislike to Vienna and the Viennese. One absurd story, to the effect that when Her Majesty entered her box at the opera, she always went in backwards, as she did not wish to bow to the audience, only shows how easily a jealous people can invent imaginary causes of discontent. It is natural enough that the Royal Family should be desirous of showing attention to a state which, after so many years of open rebellion and warfare, has now manifested every disposition to lay down the sword, and take up the plough and the navvy's spade, with the view of developing the splendid natural riches of that fertile land. Glorious, however, as is the object proposed both by the Emperor and by the Hungarian people, it is none the less true that not only the mother state of Austria, but the equally richly endowed sister land of Bohemia, are angry and jealous at the concessions granted to a country whose allegiance has been only recently recovered, and wonder why for them, also, no fatted calf is killed, and no rich robe brought forth.

For those who are fond of wild flowers, there is never-ceasing occupation and amusement at Ischl. A rich collection might be made of dried specimens with very little trouble. In many places the banks used to be quite covered with the small dark pink cyclamen, which perfumed the air for a long distance with its delicate scent. Seven sorts of gentians I found in the neighbourhood, some most lovely, like small sapphire stars; others of that large deep blue sort which we have in our gardens in England. One I observed was very like the latter species, only that it grew in clusters, on stems a foot high. A very large chocolate-coloured one, spotted with black, also attracted my notice. The rest were smaller, one being like our common wild English gentian, and the others dark indigo blue, and insignificant-looking by the side of the more beautiful kinds. There were many specimens of the rarer ferns, such as *polypodium calcarium*, and holly ferns growing in abundance. Several sorts of the graceful little pyrola, and numbers of other beautiful blossoms that were new to me, and of whose names even I was ignorant, will reward the pleasant labours of those who are eager to explore the Flora of the Austrian dominions.

In July the town was inundated with sellers of apricots and cherries. Nearly every cottage for miles round has its cherry orchard, and is covered with apricot trees, which this year were loaded with their delicious fruit, in such abundance that they were sold absurdly cheap. Figs were scarce and dear, at twopence a piece; but mountain strawberries were abundant at the same price for a soup-plate full. The wild raspberries were a failure this year, owing to the dry summer. However, they are considered feverish! How lovely the little patches of hot rocky banks look far up in the mountain fastnesses, covered with their carpet of the graceful runners of the wild strawberries, loaded with ripe scarlet fruit! The scene would make a much prettier sketch than many of the everlasting flower and fruit subjects that we see year after year in our London exhibitions, though I have often lamented that in the foreground of a landscape it would look decidedly too pre-Raphaelite.

Now I am on the subject of sketching, let me strongly recommend to travelling amateurs the new "slow-drying," moist water-colours, sold in tubes by Newman, for out-door sketching, especially under a very hot sun. They are invaluable, and extremely pleasant to work with.

Chapter V.

WALK TO THE RETTENBACH MUHLE—ACCIDENT TO A RUSSIAN
PRINCE AND HIS SON—A LOVE-STORY—HALLSTADT—
DEFORMED PEOPLE AND IDIOTS—VISIT TO OBERTRAUN—
JOURNEY INTO STYRIA—THE EINSPANNER—ALT-AUSSEE.

CHAPTER V.

THIS year has been painfully marked in Ischl by several melancholy accidents, which have at different times cast a gloom over the place. One of the first walks I took was to the Rettenbach Mühle —a favourite resort from Ischl when a few people can be found to tear themselves away from the ceaseless treadmill of the Esplanade. It is a pretty walk by the side of a stream which, falling from the mountains near Aussee, runs through a beautifully-wooded glen, and falls into the Traun at Ischl. Strong men and children are able to accomplish this expedition on foot; but as the "Mühle" is three quarters of an hour distant from the town, ladies are carried in chairs by porters—for in Ischl scarcely one of the women ever walked even the length of the Promenade.

Arrived at the mill, you can have some very good coffee and cakes, or the excellent Austrian fancy breads. It is a lovely, quiet little spot; and just above the mill the stream comes down from the mountains in a cascade, bringing with it the wood hewn on the slopes above, and thrown into the Rettenbach as logs of every size and diameter. These are stopped by a dam, of which the sluice-gates are only occasionally opened, when a good body of water is collected, which sends the accumulation of logs dashing and rolling down the stream into the Traun, where they are collected for fuel for the salt-works.

Due notice of the opening of the sluice-gates is always given, in case anyone should be wandering too near the banks, and be struck by the falling timber. Fifteen years ago a Russian Prince was nearly drowned at this spot, and this summer, about a week after my visit to the Rettenbach mill, he was again there, in company with his wife and son (an only child, fourteen years old), and the tutor. The Princess was on the bank in one of the sedan-chairs, watching her husband and son, as they looked for pebbles in the bed of the river, in which there was very little water. Due notice had been given of the opening of the sluice-gates, and they were warned to leave the rocks, as it was time for the water to come; but by some extraordinary fatality they only laughed at the warning, saying they could all swim. Presently, to the horror of the lookers-on, the pent-up body of water came sweeping down in a torrent, and all three were borne off in a moment. The Prince and tutor managed to get to the bank, but the father, not seeing his son, dashed again into the roaring water, just at the moment when the whole fearful weight of logs came thundering down. The death of father and son must have been instantaneous. The body of the former was found that night, but the poor boy's not till late next day. The appearance of both showed that they must have been at once killed by the falling timber.

The feelings of the bereaved wife and mother, helplessly sitting by and seeing, in a moment, her life made desolate for ever, are too terrible to think of. The Emperor most kindly begged her at once to go to one of his palaces, away from the scene of so much misery, and relations and friends flocked to her assistance, but it was some time before she could be moved. By a sad oversight the Prince had made no will, so that the poor widow, by the laws of Austria, only came in for a small portion of his property, and is left comparatively poor.

The next accident we heard of was to a countryman of our own, Sir Robert Phillimore, who with his son was staying at the Hotel Bauer. They had ascended a hill in the neighbourhood, and the walk having taken some time more than they expected, on their return Sir Robert suggested a short cut. When part of the descent had been accomplished, he fell, and rolled down into the darkness. With considerable difficulty his son found out his perilous position, but had to wait some time before he could make his cries for help heard by the woodmen. Sir Robert was much shaken and bruised, and for several days after was confined to his room.

In our own little household the dark shadow of death cast its gloom over these bright summer days. We had noticed that the pretty and tidy Austrian girl who waited on us grew gradually less cheerful and bright. Her large dark eyes often showed unmistakeable symptoms that she had been indulging in violent fits of crying. If we inquired what was the matter, she invariably replied, "Oh! it is nothing—nothing." Had the landlady scolded her? "Oh! no." Was she ill? "No." At last, one morning, after having brought in our breakfast, and set it down, she caught hold of C——— by the arm, and burst forth with a torrent of tears. What was it? we asked, rather amazed at this unexpected outburst of grief. "Oh! he is dead!—he is dead!" was all she could sob out.

After she had calmed down a little, she told us, with tears still flowing from her eyes, that it was her lover. He had been a trumpeter in a cavalry regiment, and had long suffered from lung disease (that fearfully prevalent malady in Austria). In the first spring days he had been granted leave to come home to his family in Ischl to be taken care of. To get well again, as they hoped; to die, as it proved. Poor Fanny! the red eyes and sad looks for which she would not account, were the results of her sad visits to her dying lover. She had been to see him the evening before, and they had promised to send for her in the night if he was worse; but the summons had come very softly, and the young soldier had passed away in his sleep.

A family of Prussians were recently hastily summoned away by the intelligence that a brother had been thrown from his carriage and seriously hurt. Before they got far on their journey another telegram reached them to say he was dead. A foreign doctor in one of the hotels also dropped down dead, and a Count of Austria died from a cancer in the mouth, caused only by a burn from a cigar. In short, funeral processions were constantly passing, and the funeral march was frequently heard. In such a small place it seemed very dreary, and I was extremely glad to start with a friend on a little expedition into Styria.

We went the first day to Hallstadt, not very far from Ischl; but the heat was too great to allow of much travelling. Hallstadt is a very picturesque little village, perched on ledges of rock, and built down so close to the edge of the lake, that the base of most of the dwellings terminates in a boat-house; boats here taking the place of carts and wheel-barrows. Hallstadt is nearly spoilt by a very ugly new church, and by crowds of tourists, who swarm in all the little inns. These visitors enjoy the views in sedan-chairs, or feed the fish in the lake from the numerous summer-houses that the inn gardens contain.

If the views of lake, mountain, and waterfall are lovely about Hallstadt, most certainly the inhabitants are not; and it makes one's heart sick to see the number of idiots, horribly deformed people, and dwarfs that you meet at every turn. It is perfectly appalling to think that only about every third person is like a rational, full-grown human being. A gentleman whom I met there, who had travelled far and wide, said in all his journeys he had never seen such a stricken place, except in some of the leper towns in Sweden. It really seems as if the curse of some fearful sentence was on Hallstadt.

We took a boat from Hallstadt, and were rowed over the lake to a cluster of cottages, I believe called Obertraun. On the way we were shown a cross erected by the side of the lake, where a boat full of holiday peasants was upset, and all in it drowned, by the sudden descent of one of those mountain hurricanes which make the Hallstadt one of the most dangerous lakes for boats in all Austria. Tourists may therefore rejoice over the small steamer which plies several times a day between Hallstadt and the two landing places at the north-end.

When we landed at Obertraun we had to wait for a conveyance, as all the village was haymaking. Our Jehu was a highly respectable and no doubt opulent farmer, who came somewhat unwillingly from his work, and harnessed his good stout horse into his Einspanner cart. At first we went along rather moodily, the farmer casting regretful glances back at his merry band of hay-makers.

Presently, however, a sudden grip in the road sent us all with a bound into the air, and made us both burst out with a hearty laugh, in which the farmer joined, and we immediately fraternised. He told us he had given twenty pounds for his horse, such a capital, strong beast, with a glossy black coat. At the end of the journey we were quite sorry to part, and he agreed at some future time to make a long trip into Styria with us.

The first hour of our drive was through orchard-meadows, only a narrow strip, with walls of lofty mountains on each side; and before us, at the end of the glen, a still more forbidding-looking precipice of dark rock. Where the outlet to this valley, which was to lead us into Styria was, we could not imagine. At last, almost over our heads, I espied a mountain road along a ledge of rock.

"Impossible!" said my companion.

"There is no other way out that I can see," I meekly answered.

And, accordingly, we had not gone much further before our farmer drew up, and said he must beg us to walk only a quarter of an hour. Accordingly, out we got, very loth, for it was twelve o'clock, and the sun was blazing down with a beating heat that was quite overpowering.

Of course the road perversely went on the sunny side of the glen; while on the other side we could see, through openings of the luxuriant, magnificent trees, great patches of snow still lying on the ground. It looked so temptingly cold, and seemed so near, that one fancied he could almost reach over and cool his hands in it. At the bottom of the glen, the mountain torrent tossed and foamed along, bearing the fir logs, which men were busily engaged in cutting on the tops of the mountain.

About half way up we passed a slide, where watchers were stationed to warn those above when carts or passengers were passing. Before us toiled horse and farmer, dragging the light cart over rough rocks and broken ground, which looked more like the dry bed of a torrent than the "good road" which the faithless "Murray" had promised us. However, when the quarter of an hour had increased to nearly three, we had reached the summit, and were thankful to seat ourselves once more in the Einspanner. This is a most wonderful light carriage quite peculiar to Austria, and one on which the people pride themselves extremely. It consists of any sort of light carriage, with a pole instead of shafts; and the one horse is always harnessed to the near side of the pole. It has a most unpleasant appearance, suggesting the idea that the fellow horse had suddenly dropped down dead, and been left at the road-side; or that the proprietors of the equipage had started in life with more exalted notions than they were afterwards able to realize. It is in vain to ask why the cart is so constructed, for they will give you twenty answers, and each with as little common sense as the others. They will tell you that the roads are so bad, that the horse goes better by the side; that it is easier to guide; that the pole is more convenient for mountain travelling than the shafts; and so on. I can only say that it is difficult to imagine the invention of anything so awkward and ugly.

After our tedious ascent, the road was shady and delightful, passing under firwoods the whole way to Aussee, which is a great salt-working place. We drove on to Alt-Aussee, and took up our quarters at the hotel on the lake. Here we found very rough accommodation; and, moreover, it was enormously dear. We were abundantly repaid, however, by the glorious view of the glaciers and snowy peaks of the

Dachstein, seen at some distance over fields and hills of fir-wood, with the beautiful lake of Alt-Aussee as a foreground. We ought to have gone on and seen two other small lakes, which are well worth visiting; but it really was so overpoweringly hot, that we could not find any pleasure in either walking or boating (the only means by which the upper lakes are reached.) We remained, therefore, quietly at Alt-Aussee, watching the bright sunshine and green shadows on the far-away snow-fields of the splendid Dachstein.

Chapter VI.

EBENSEE—THE INN AND THE WATER-MILL—KING AND QUEEN OF HANOVER—THE SALT-WORKS—PROCESS OF MANUFACTURE—CONDITION OF THE WORKMEN—HERR VON PRINZIGER—MUMMY CHILDREN—A SUGGESTION TO BARON VON BEUST.

CHAPTER VI.

THE Lake of Ebensee, or Traunsee, or Gmündenersee, as it is variously called, is only two hours from Ischl, and a few days at the little village inn of the Post at Ebensee pass very pleasantly. The scenery is beautiful, and comprises all one can desire for the perfection of a quiet mountain landscape. There are no grand and overpowering beauties like those of the Tyrol or Switzerland, but the town is picturesque—a dark green lake, and chains of fine mountains closing round on all sides. The inn, too, is clean and comfortable, especially in hot weather, when you can dine and sup out of doors, thereby avoiding the overpowering fumes of bad tobacco, which here, as everywhere in Austria, destroys all comfort in the public rooms.

I must especially warn all my friends, if they can, to avoid room No. 16. We arrived on Sunday morning, and found the inn very full. There was only one room to be had, to which we were shown. It was a very large one, nicely furnished, very clean, and with seven windows at least. We took possession of it gladly, and after going to church, walked about the town.

In the afternoon, after dinner, we rowed across the lake, and took a walk to a very pretty waterfall in the midst of a thick pine-wood. We thus had had a good deal of walking, and by ten o'clock were glad to go to bed and to sleep. About three in the morning (I know it seemed to me as if I had only just fallen asleep), there began the most fearful and distracting noise exactly at our bed-heads, which roused us with a start from our peaceful slumbers. The sound was a combination of groaning, creaking, grinding, sawing, and splashing, forcibly suggesting to us the most unpleasant truth that we were next-door neighbours to a saw and flour mill, turned by one of the mountain streams. In the hot summer weather, the noise coming through the seven open windows, and continuing all day without intermission, and nearly all night, was really distracting. Millers do not leave off work when other well-regulated establishments cease from the labours of the day, but carry on their noisy operations far into the night by the light of tallow ·candles. In consequence of the annoying uproar we could hardly hear each other speak. I found out afterwards that the room is well known to experienced travellers, and those who know the country, and by such prudently avoided. Except for this, the inn was very comfortable. It was under the active superintendence of a good bustling landlady, who was everywhere at once, and yet never too busy to answer any questions.

When we arrived first, there were standing close to the inn three open carriages, with the Royal scarlet liveries of England. These contained the King and Queen of Hanover, and the two Princesses, their daughters, with their attendants. They put up at the Post, and had dinner in the courtyard in front. The people about behaved so well, no crowding or staring. Only on the other side of the courtyard a group of peasants in their Sunday clothes assembled in breathless silence, to watch a King and Queen eat their dinner. We met them afterwards in our walk, and could not but look with admiration on the Queen, who had given the Prussians, in 1866, more trouble than all the other crowned heads put together, and who clung to her lost kingdom and home with a determination which, though useless, was wonderfully brave. The King looks very old for his years. His hair is perfectly white, and he is very bald, but his figure is quite erect, and he has a proud bearing. The two Princesses are tall and pretty, and extremely graceful.

The Royal Family of Hanover were staying at the Château of Ebenzweier, which belonged to the Archduke Maximilian. The German papers said that the king was advised to leave Vienna during the rifle meeting, as the Hanoverians yet delight in showing their loyalty and affection to the sovereign whom they still long for, and in these times of peace all demonstrations are to be avoided. I suppose it was to further this excellent object that the soldiers in Vienna formed three deep round the Lancers at the People's Ball after the shooting festival.

We had a very kind friend at Ebensee in Herr von Prinzinger, the government manager of the salt-works there. These works are very large, and employ a great number of hands. The first salt-works in these parts were erected at Hallstadt, when the demand became so great that they were soon found too small. Others were then constructed at Ischl, and when more were required, these at Ebensee were built. The salt is run in a liquid state from Hallstadt by pipes along the mountains to Ischl and Ebensee—a process which is found cheaper and more economical, as respects fuel and carriage, than the enlargement of the original works at the mine's mouth at Hallstadt would be.

We had been over the salt-mines at Berchtesgaden, and were also very anxious to see these salt-works, which Herr von Prinzinger at once offered to show us over. We were first taken to the top of the high building, and shown the taps and tanks into which the brine runs by a clever contrivance. The liquid, as it falls, marks off on a dial the number of measures filled in the day. An overlooker has charge of these taps, and if one fails running, it is traced back to the fault in the wooden pipes that convey the brine from the mine.

Very often, when taking a walk along the

footpath between Hallstadt and Ischl, or Ischl and Ebensee, we came across a loose plank lying in the ground. If this was raised, we could see the wooden pipes running under the road on which we were walking. These places are for the convenience of the men who inspect the pipes to see if repairs are wanting. There are also at intervals small wooden huts, where they keep their tools, and a supply of such materials as are necessary in their work. The brine runs from the tanks and measures at the top of the building into very large reservoirs of iron, firmly fixed in frames of strong brickwork over ovens in which wood is burnt. These fires are kept constantly supplied with logs of wood, and the water above is maintained at boiling pitch.

At each end of these reservoirs stand four or five men, on a raised platform, to bring them within three feet of the edge of the caldron of boiling brine. They are each provided with a long-handled shovel, with which they lift the salt from the bottom, and throw it down wooden troughs into long rows of pails which stand about six feet below. The shovellers are followed step by step by men with very long-handled wooden rakes, with which they keep drawing the salt from the centre towards the edges, where it is more easy to reach. Men with wooden shoes stand in the pails below, and, as the hot salt is poured in, stamp it down. I may here remark that the shoes are scrupulously clean, and kept entirely for this work. Herr von Prinzinger significantly pointed out to our notice a row of the ordinary shoes left inside the door till the work of their proprietors was over.

The pails, when filled, are carried to hot closets, where they are kept till the salt is perfectly dried, when the loaves are turned out and piled up in a large storehouse. It was curious to see the incrustations of Glauber salt which ooze out, and form large masses, after the salt is cold, and even stored—sometimes quite covering the loaves with all sorts of fantastic incrustations. None of the salt is what we should consider first quality in England, being a dirty yellowish white, and certainly never possessing the pungent taste to which we are accustomed. Much is also thrown about and spilled in the process of making, which is considered very clumsy and defective.

As salt is a royal monopoly in Austria, and it would not answer to allow even the poor people to buy refuse at a cheaper rate, the waste salt is mixed with some preparation of iron, which colours it bright orange, when the peasant will no longer buy it. This does not injure it, however, for the royal cattle, or deer, are fed with this mixed in their food.

The ovens of this vast building are on the ground floor, and men are kept continually employed feeding them with huge logs of wood, as they burn constantly for ten days at once. At the end of that time the fires are let out, and the pan above is allowed to cool, when it is cleared out, and any cracks or fissures are carefully searched for.

The men are paid partly in money and partly by rations—bread, lard, butter, and grain, which the Emperor retails cheaply to them. They are well paid for Austria. Every child in their families is taken into account, and for every fresh arrival they have extra pay. They also retire on a pension after a long service. Including wood-cutters, boatmen, wood-pipe makers, and actual workers, about six hundred men are employed in the salt-works at Ebensee. It is hard labour, but very healthy, the men rarely having any illness. Herr von Prinzinger seems greatly beloved amongst them. We were told in the village that he had done very much to improve the condition of the workmen in every respect. He has obtained for them a better quality of bread, has established schools for their children, and encouraged the musical abilities of the men by the formation of a band. In short, he is one of the few Austrians who march with the times, and do not sigh over the departure of everything old-fashioned and belonging to the " good old days," as if the world were "going to the dogs." Modern refinements and elegancies are not superfluous follies in his eyes, as his tastefully-arranged house plainly shows.

Whilst I was at Ebensee not only did I satisfy my curiosity about the salt-works, but I also had the gratification of holding in my hands a real live mummy baby! It is a most wonderful circumstance, but you may reside any time in a German village, and while holding daily intercourse with inhabitants of every age and size, yet never see a baby! In the cool of the evening most of the women come out and spin or knit at their doors, while pale, sickly-looking children crawl about them; but among them you never, by any chance, see a baby. This curious fact, I suppose, is owing to the mummy system of baby-nursing.

As our landlady possesses a baby of six months old, attired in the orthodox mummy fashion, I had an opportunity of examining its bands and wrappings, and can faithfully describe them. The little helpless creature is first clad in some of the usual baby under-garments, and then is tightly bound by swathes of linen to a quilted hard wrapper, in which it is encased like a chrysalis, its legs being so bound that it cannot move them. This wrapper, after being again bound very tightly round, is ornamented with a ribbon and bow—a wretched mockery of the poor little sufferer. Until quite recently the arms also were confined in the same rigid way. If the poor babies could only speak, how indignantly would they denounce that "tyrant custom," which thus deprives them of their natural liberty. With what eloquence would they express their amazement that in this enlightened nineteenth century *their* mothers should be the slaves of such ignorant prejudices. And with what bitter sarcasm would they turn to their general mother, Alemannia, and ask her why, instead of wandering in the dreamland of metaphysical speculation, she did not at once open her eyes, and on a subject of so much philanthropic interest deign to take a hint from practical England.

When a baby is thus made into a bundle, and a bit of moist white bread tied into a rag is popped into its mouth, it can be left for hours by itself, like the North American's papooses, and gives no trouble to anyone. The only drawback—and it is a rather serious one—is that the number of deformed children is something truly appalling. If the unfortunate mummy draws up a leg, or gets a twist by unskilled swathing, it is sure to turn crooked in limb or body. In the little village of Brunn, during my stay there this summer, three unfortunate mummy babies under four months old, all born perfectly straight, had to undergo surgical treatment in consequence of crooked legs and spines. With the cottagers very often, as with us, an elder sister—herself only a child—is left to act as nurse, at an age when so young a girl cannot be expected to see the necessity of swathing a baby perfectly straight; and if the little victim does not lie quite still in a horizontal position when undergoing the ordeal, a little limb is soon twisted, and the child is crippled for life.

This disgusting practice is continued for the first six months of their life, and during the next half year they have long robes like our babies. At the end of the first year, if they can walk, the boys have corduroy trowsers, waistcoat, and jackets, and usually a blue apron. It is quite distressing to see little roly-poly children, just able to toddle about, dressed up like figures in a pantomime, with their pale, weird faces and lank, colourless hair in keeping with their strange attire. Only twice this year have I seen pretty, rosy, healthy children! When I return to England, the first thing that strikes me is always the healthy beauty and joyous look of the village children.

The Emperor and Baron von Beust had lately introduced some excellent minor reforms into Austria. It would tell well in the growth of the next generation, if mummy babies were abolished by law. I was thankful to get rid of our landlady's, it was so uncomfortable to hold. I had an almost uncontrollable wish to break it in half, and make it sit down or bend. It reminded me forcibly of one of those dolls which in our young days we used to receive as presents with great contempt, unnatural-looking figures, with unpliable wooden legs and arms, stiff and unjointed, which we could regard with no motherly affection.

In German there is no equivalent for the English word "baby." The unfortunates are generally called "Kleine Kinder" (little children), or "Wickel-Kinder" (rolled up children). The nursery is the "Kinds Zimmer" (child's room), and the nurse is "Kinds Frau" (child's woman). None of these words convey the home-like comfortable ideas that our English ones do.

"If the rolled-up child is not asleep, let us go into the child's room, and ask the child's woman for some tea," does not sound half so cosy as "Let us go into the nursery, and if baby is not asleep we will ask nurse for a cup of tea."

Chapter VII.

FLOATING DOWN TIMBER—DESTRUCTION OF A VILLAGE BY FIRE—COOKING SALMON—A DANCE IN THE INN—THE EMPEROR AS A SPORTSMAN—TROUT PRESERVE—THE LANDLADY AT THE KRAHE—SHOOTING LODGE AT OFFENSEE—THE VIRGINIAN CREEPER AND THE TEA-PLANT—AN IMPERIAL HUNTSMAN.

CHAPTER VII.

IN the evening we walked down to the vast timber-yard at the edge of the lake, where the timber is stored for burning in the salt-works. The wood is all floated down from the mountains by the river Traun, which is often choked up for a long distance by the accumulated logs. The people are dreadfully lazy and careless of this splendid timber, and it is often allowed to lie so long in the water, that it is half rotten before the proper official orders it to be taken out to the sawing mills. It seems such a pity to cut up those magnificent trees, with which they usually feed their fires.

When one thinks that there is a cheap and easy water-road all the way from most of the forest mountains, high and broad streams that run into the Danube, by which any quantity of timber could be easily floated down to many parts of Hungary, where roads are scarce, and where it would be most valuable, it seems a pity that it should be allowed to lie and rot in the small tributary stream.

The wooden planks of most floors in common rooms in Austria measure on an average twenty-five inches wide, while many are thirty inches broad. The houses, too, are everywhere roofed with wood, which looks extremely pretty, as it is often painted, and with age takes various colours. It is fearfully dangerous, however, and when once a fire breaks out in a village, what with the wooden roofs and the quantity of hay and dry fodder that the inhabitants store in the "Boden," or loft of their houses, there is little chance of extinguishing it, especially in a dry summer like the last, so that you hear of the conflagration of entire villages.

When we were in Brünn one evening at eight o'clock, the servants rushed in to beg us to come out on the balcony, and look at a fearful fire that was raging in the distance. It was a long way off, but the whole heavens were crimson, like a glorious sunset. The fire soon died away, but next morning we heard that the entire village of Aspern, on the Danube, had been burnt in the short space of two hours, the church towers only being left standing. The inhabitants were very poor people, chiefly employed at the new iron manufactories at Simmering. When I inquired for particulars, which I often did, it was wonderful to me how calmly the Brünn people treated such a catastrophe. Perhaps it was too common an occurrence for them to trouble themselves much about it, or probably they were too near Vienna to think of anything so *triste* and dispiriting as human calamity and misery. However, if Aspern is to be rebuilt, it will not run the chance of such a misfortune again, as by one of the excellent modern reform laws it is no longer legal to roof new erections of any sort, in town or country, with wood. Old wooden roofs may still be repaired with the same material, and consequently many of the Hungarian, Bohemian, and Styrian villages will long look beautifully picturesque, but, alas! sadly unsafe.

All this time, however, we are left sitting on the timber by Ebensee. We are sketching the lake and mountains as quickly as we can, so as to be ready to seize the exact moment to colour them when the setting sun, for only five minutes before it sinks, lights up the face of the limestone mountains with the most exquisite blush of deep rose-colour, but so transient that it must be at once put on paper.

After the sun had gone down, the fleecy clouds that overhung the tops of the lofty Traunstein and Erlerkogel, were illuminated by the same beautiful tint of pale crimson, whilst the surrounding mountains were reflected in the dark lake a deep iron grey. The scene was so quiet and enjoyable, that it was difficult to tear oneself away from it. How beautiful was the changing sky!—how imposing those mountains that looked down on the lake, sleeping so calmly, and rippled now and then by a few fishing boats, or by some of the heavy logs of wood floated down by the Traun!

A chain is moored on the surface of the

lake, not far from the mouth of the river, over which the steamer and fishing boats glide easily, but which prevents the logs from escaping too far into the lake. There is very good fishing here, and salmon are constantly caught, but are generally sent to the Vienna market. They have a peculiar fashion of cooking them at Ebensee by taking the flesh out of the skin, and putting it in again, mashed up with potatoes, onions, and parsley.

We spent several very pleasant days at Ebensee, taking either little excursions to see the neighbouring lakes, or enjoying beautiful walks round the mountain village. One morning we chanced to come on a little inn in a retired spot, where there were music and dancing going on. After partaking of some delicious coffee, we took a peep at the ball-room. What the dance was called, I cannot pretend to say; but the men seemed a party of tradesmen, or officials, probably from Gmünden; while their partners were chosen from the prettiest among the groups of peasant women who were gathered round. They began by dancing slowly round the room arm-in-arm; then the music got quicker, and the "lady" followed her partner with her hands on his shoulders. The music being played still quicker, they whirled round, with their arms twirling over each other's head. A very rapid valse then followed, concluded by the gentleman whirling his partner as high in the air as his strength of arm would permit.

All this time a poor travelling pedlar, who had only an hour or two before formed one of the party, was lying dead in a house close by! He was well known by the peasants as one who wandered about the country with his wares. A gentleman this evening had given him a larger coin than he usually received, and he seemed so delighted that it was supposed the excitement had brought on an attack of heart complaint, from which he dropped down dead. Yet the peasants went on with their music and dancing as if nothing had happened.

A charming drive from Ebensee is that which takes us by a beautiful mountain road, in excellent order, to Langbathsee, where the Emperor has a hunting-lodge, at which he was expected the day after we were there. The mountains round abound in game, and there are glades cut in the forests that surround the house, through which the deer are driven for the royal party to shoot. The Emperor is a keen sportsman, and the people speak enthusiastically of his skill in shooting, his zeal in the chase, and his endurance in pursuit of chamois. No mountain daunts him; and he will climb places where many of his Jäger dare not follow. The longest summer day does not appear too long for him to pursue his favourite sport. The little Prince Imperial seems also inclined to follow his father's example, and though only ten years old, has already been out several times, and shot well too.

There is a large open space of lawn round the shooting-lodge, to which, in the early summer mornings, the chamois often come down in herds to feed. It is a very pretty, quiet spot, with the small lake in front, and round it fine mountains. There is a beautiful walk through a wood at the back of the house, which leads you to a very quiet, dark little lake, nestled under the side of the heavy frowning precipices and beetling craigs which overhang it, but fringed round with bright tender green beeches, and a many-coloured carpet of wild flowers—such lovely blue gentians, wild asphodels, monkshood, and beds of forget-me-nots. In the shallow waters multitudes of small fishes swam about, and under the bridge some good-sized trout were basking. I suppose the sight of these made us think of dinner, for we instantly began retracing our steps to the spot on the other side of Langbathsee where our carriage was waiting.

We drove to the "Krähe," a little inn of moderate pretensions, but with a character in the person of the landlady, and with a tank of excellent trout. Meat was not to be thought of; but we had a large dish of plain boiled trout, some smoking-hot potatoes, excellent butter and black bread. Generally they spoil the trout by boiling them with some vinegar in the water to harden the flesh, a process which certainly destroys the delicate taste. The landlady did not use vinegar, or very little, and her trout were some of the best I have ever eaten.

After dinner we went down to the tank to see the trout preserve, which was filled by a little mountain stream. The fish, which seem to live very comfortably, are principally fed on the small fish caught in the shallows; but when these are not to be had, they give them raw liver minced very fine. Near Ischl there are very large tanks for trout and saibling. In these they are sorted according to size, where space can allow of it; an excellent arrangement, for in the mountain tanks very often the biggest fish get the lion's share, and the smaller ones fare badly.

The landlady at the "Krähe" was a very chatty old body, and very communicative. She had lived there a great many years, and though the place was so retired and solitary, she said that even in winter it was not dull, as the woodcutters and herdsmen generally dropped in every evening to smoke their pipes and drink beer. For her better half she had a profound contempt, which she did not scruple to express by significant shrugs and sneers whenever he was referred to.

The girl who waited on us had her face tied up, suffering from a bad toothache. The old landlady remarked *she* never suffered from toothache; she had had her teeth all taken out. On our observing it was not particularly becoming to go without teeth, she said, if she had been younger, she would have thought more of it; but now it did not signify.

We said,

"But your husband, surely he does not like it; what does he think?"

"Oh! as to that, I don't mind the least. If he wishes me to do what pleases me, then I do it; but if he wishes me to do what I do not like, then I leave it alone!"

Truly, that little solitary inn on the lake side must never be dull. It would not, however, be the cheerfulness of the inmates that would rouse up the spirit of animation, but the stimulating effect of the keen tongue of the landlady.

The Emperor had another shooting lodge near Ebensee, but in a contrary direction to Langbathsee, on the little lake of Offen. The road to it is like all the roads about, most beautiful, only varied in one spot by an ascent up the side of a mountain nearly as steep as the walls of a house. The horse found a difficulty in dragging even the light Einspanner up some bits of it. The driver did not suggest our walking, and till the horse began to jib he did not see the necessity. On our return, mountain "Arabs" were lying in wait with ropes, with the aid of which, the wheels being all securely fastened together, the carriage slid down this hill. I need not say we seized the earliest opportunity to get out and walk down.

The Kaiser's shooting-lodge at Offensee is very pretty, and as we had a card of introduction to the head Jäger, we went all over it. It is so nicely furnished, and reminded me of a shooting-lodge in Scotland. In the one sitting room all the furniture, even to the chairs and chandelier, is made of deers' horns. Old engravings of sporting subjects hang round the room, and in a recess stands a very well-furnished bookcase, in which I noticed German translations of many of Fenimore Cooper's tales and novels. A large boat-house stands near the lodge, containing a good many boats, longer and lighter than the usual boats which they use on the lakes in Austria.

It is well worth rowing out into the middle of the Offensee to see a beautiful view of mountain tops, which nearer in shore are hidden by the hills covered with pine woods, in which splendid specimens of capercailzie are sometimes shot. Some of these birds, of magnificent plumage and size, have been photographed and coloured, and now adorn the walls of the lodge. The Jäger who showed us over the place spoke, like the others, most enthusiastically of the Emperor's love of sport, and of the abundance of game about. He said there was very little poaching here, but more on the Styrian border. The whole of the Salzkammergut is exclusively an Imperial shooting monopoly, and splendid sport it must afford. The lodge had a pretty attempt at a small garden, mostly on rock-work. The usual Virginian creeper was growing most luxuriantly. I never saw it grow in England as it does here. It is usually covered with bunches of black grapes, very small and hard, which obtain for it in this country the name of wild vine. There is another little shrub, rather common in England, called the tea-plant, which grows all through the summer and autumn. With us it has lilac and brown blossoms, insignificant and scentless. In Austria there are hedges of it, and late in summer the sprays are covered with masses of orange-coloured berries, like small capsicums, which fully compensate for the want of beauty in the flower.

Our survey of the Royal demesne did not take very long; but it certainly is a very pleasant thing for poor travellers to find themselves in a country where an Imperial huntsman will spend half an hour showing you over a Royal residence, and afterwards row you out on the lake, and receive less than two shillings English money with boundless gratitude!

Chapter VIII.

LINZ—MILITARY MUSIC—AUSTRIAN UNIFORM—PROMOTION IN THE ARMY—PETTY JEALOUSIES—RECRUITING—WOMEN EMPLOYED AS LABOURERS—NAVIGATION OF THE DANUBE—SCENERY ON ITS BANKS—MILITARY CADETS—KISSING AND SHAKING HANDS—VIENNA.

CHAPTER VIII.

VERY glad was I to say good-bye to the promenade at Ischl, with its indifferent band and weary treadmill of Viennese shopkeepers, and to find myself on the way to Linz, through the fine mountain pass to Ebensee. We went by steamer down the lake to Gmunden, where we got into the train, and arrived at Linz at four. There is nothing in any way to interest one in Linz, and it is rather pleasant to arrive at a town where one can rest in peace, and not be obliged to submit to the penance of going out to see churches and picture-galleries. The name of Linz, therefore, remains in my mind associated with the most calm and peaceful reminiscences.

In the evening, we heard from the balcony of the hotel some agreeable music from the band of the 11th (Crown Prince Albert of Saxony's) Infantry regiment. There were more than forty performers, and they played beautifully a very nice selection of opera and dance music; but they were almost too near and loud for us to enjoy it thoroughly. One of the brothers of the Emperor, the Archduke Karl Ludwig, was in the same balcony with us, having supper, and the band remained till he left.

I am afraid this year is the last time I shall see the pretty white uniforms, as a new regulation has come out, in virtue of which they are all to be changed to dark blue. Formerly all the Austrian infantry regiments of the line had white uniforms, with different-coloured facings—a dress which dated from the Crusades. The scarlet shield of Austria, with the white stripe on it, derived its origin from the fact that Leopold the Glorious in the Holy Land wore a white uniform, with a broad gold sash round his waist. After a hard day's fighting, when he returned to his tent, his white coat was red with the blood of the slain; and as he took off his sash, a white band was left where the belt had covered his uniform. From that time the scarlet shield with the white band became the arms of Austria, and the soldiers have ever since worn white coats. However, as this is no age of romance, but of practical reality, this ancient uniform is now to be discontinued. Though one cannot but regret the change, it must be allowed there are good reasons for it. It was a constant employment to keep the uniform clean, and the white tunic was a conspicuous mark for the enemy in war-time. Since the last war, many a solitary grave lying round the great battle-fields is passed with the remark, "That was thanks to the white uniform;" for the sentries or pickets who, in grey or dark colours, might have escaped the observation of the enemy, afforded in their white coats an easy mark to men armed with the needle-guns, in any light, and to an incredible distance. It is devoutly to be hoped that the day when Austria shall again be obliged to unsheath the sword is far distant; but in this new uniform, and with so effective an arm as the breechloader which all the Austrian soldiers now carry, the army would certainly be better prepared than it was in 1866; though whether the generals are now better qualified for the command of large bodies of troops than they were then, is, I fear, still a doubtful question.

Promotion in the Austrian army is still decided too much by rank and favouritism. A young man with a title, even though his education may be so imperfect that he cannot spell correctly, is set over the heads of old officers, who are not only, like Cassio, learned in the "bookish theorick" of war, but who have acquired military skill and the art of command by experience in the battle-field. It is the " curse of service " that

> " Preferment goes by letter and affection,
> Not by the old gradation."

The gilded favourites of fortune, who

> " Never set a squadron in the field
> Nor the division of a battle know
> More than a spinster"—

—men whose soldiership is mere " prattle without practice," step over veterans who have fought in more campaigns than they can number years; and thus it is that soldiers who have given proof of their warlike skill on many a well-fought field—probably neither at Rhodes nor at Cyprus, yet "on other grounds, christen'd and heathen"—are "belee'd and becalmed" by mere "popinjays"—to use the expression of Hotspur—who, if they are only of noble birth, may know no more of military strategy than " the tongued consuls."

Since Baron von Beust, however, has been Prime Minister, the Royal saloons have been thrown open to a mixture of ranks that must have curdled the blood of the exclusive aristocrats with horror at such a contamination; but as they have survived it, it is to be hoped that they have not felt any evil effects from His Majesty's gracious condescension to his lower subjects. Let us hope, therefore, that gradually this discernment of worth and talent in people not born with the blue blood of countless generations may extend to the army and general society, so that the ignorant prejudice and narrow-minded exclusiveness which has kept Austria so backward in her position amongst nations, may, with the days of the Concordat, soon come to be smiled at as a memorial of the dark ages of this empire.

The soldiers, unfortunately, are as well aware as any of their officers of the little jealousies and petty differences that so lamentably disqualify their leaders, and in an emergency expose the army to destruction. In relation to the last war, they talk openly of one general who sacrificed his soldiers to prove that another was wrong in his tactics. At Skalitz, when they saw that the fight had turned against them, and that the day would be lost if the reserve force did not come up quickly, the general of the latter body, who had a spite of his own against the commander, purposely led his men by the longest route to the relief of their comrades, and every soldier amongst them not only saw that they would be too late, but knew the cause. They will tell you that they were marched here and there without rhyme or reason, till they were thoroughly worn out and disgusted. The orders one general gave were countermanded the next hour by another. It is no longer concealed that they were in a state of utter despair and hopelessness before Königgrätz, having lost all confidence in their leaders. The soldiers audibly murmured, asking one another why they should be killed to gratify the private pique of their generals. I am afraid even Benedek himself was not free from this fault. An acquaintance of my own commanded a brigade during the war, and a most useful and well-trained regiment was suddenly detached from his command. A council of war was held shortly after, and during their discussions a friend happened to remark to the general, "So you have lost the —— regiment." "Yes," was the answer, "and more's the pity." He looked up and saw that Benedek, who had overheard this remark, was displeased, his eyes flashing angrily. Next morning the general was ordered away on some unimportant service.

The army is now on its peace footing of 300,000 men; but most people in Austria think it might be still further reduced, not only without detriment to the service of the country, but with great advantage to agriculture, as there is a fearful drain on the labouring population by the blood-tax, as they call it. Already men enough cannot be found to make up the number called out every year for military service. The officers commanding in the different districts, who have the charge of the recruiting, have by some means or other to meet the demands of the "blood-tax," to keep up the enormous standing army.

All youths over nineteen, whatsoever their rank, class, or employment, are liable to enlistment, provided they have no radical defects, are tall enough, and not flat-footed. I am not aware if in England this last peculiarity is an impediment to men desirous of entering the army; but in Austria they are so particular about it, that unless the impression of the foot, dipped in water, leaves the requisite dry mark where the arch of the instep has escaped the wet, they are rejected. If they are accepted, and by the new law there is no alternative, and they are neither able nor willing to pay the thousand gulden (which is the lowest sum accepted as smart-money), they serve for three years. If there is no war at the end of that time, and they wish it, they return home. These men generally swell the vast army of beggars in Germany. Not disposed to remain soldiers, and too idle to work at home, they roam about, extracting kreutzers from the soft-hearted, and living a dissolute, vagabond life. Everywhere in Austria these three-year soldiers bear the worst of characters. Of course if a young man of nineteen has been just taken from a trade he was learning, or from a farmstead or manufacture where he was of use and importance, it is different. If they prefer soldiering, they remain in the service for six years; and, in time of peace, remain for two years in the reserve force, which, in many respects, is equivalent to our militia. At the end of eight years (from the age of nineteen) they are free for ever.

All this soldiering is dreadfully injurious to the agricultural, and even moral prospects of the country. The women have to leave their homes and families and do the hard work of men; and it is revolting to see the peasant women transformed into horrible-looking objects, employed as scavengers, ostlers, and ploughmen. Women may even be seen thrashing and mowing, looking coarse, masculine, and brutal. Manual work of the hardest kind falls on these unfortunate creatures, for nowhere in Austria have I seen any mitigation of labour in the shape of steam help; though often in Bodenbach I used to see luggage trains pass, with engines carefully covered, on trucks from Ransome and other well-known engineering firms. I suppose, as they were going south, they were to be eventually employed somewhere in Austria, and not put into a museum!—but I have never seen one working! And all this time you see thousands upon thousands of idle soldiers loitering about in every village and town in the empire. If the Emperor could only be persuaded to give up his favourite toy, or even consent to reduce it to more reasonable bounds, it would be an unspeakable relief to the country.

We had to leave Linz at 8 A.M., by the Danube steamer, a very good boat, heavily laden with goods, and carrying a large number of passengers. The scenery is flat, and not very interesting for many miles after you pass Linz—merely a few wooded hills on each side, and shoals upon shoals of mountain sand and gravel blocking up the greater part of the stream of the noble river. The sudden bends and turns the steamer had to make to avoid these banks were marvellous—sometimes steering quite close to one side of the river, and the next minute going right across the stream and passing for some distance within a couple of feet of the opposite bank. The wash of the vessel, as we passed the shoals, carried away with its tiny waves masses of the sand and stones. In many places large patches of the tall reeds came sweeping down into the water. If this happens every time a large steamer passes, surely the bed of the river will very soon be choked up, and it will no longer be navigable.

I am told that, after some years of discussion and planning, steps are to be immediately adopted for improving the present state of the Danube. It will cost some millions of gulden, but anything is better than the present melancholy aspect of the dreary wastes of sandbanks, which render the river almost useless. The labour of removing the shoals and deepening the shallows will employ many hundred of hard-working *women!* I conclude that the times at which the large steamers pass are pretty well known in the different localities on the banks; for if not, it must be very dangerous not only for the small fishing-boats, but for those employed cutting reeds at the sides.

At many places I saw the boats drawn up high out of the wash by the poor people to whom they belonged; but at one spot I observed a boat with an old man in it, which another was holding by a rope from the beach. They had not drawn it up high enough, for the wave following us took it broadside on, and rolled it over and over. This was an accident to which they were perhaps used, for the old man clung on with a strong grip, and rolled over with the boat, seeming to suffer no harm but the wetting. The whirlpools I was prepared to find much more awful than they really are, but the scenery about them is really beautiful; and in the evening, under the effect of light and shade produced by the setting sun, it must for many miles be very striking. Under a hot August sun at midday it certainly loses much of its beauty, and I must confess to having felt disappointed.

The Rhine causes the same feeling of disappointment, even in the most beautiful parts, when seen by a noonday sun. From the railway it is almost ugly, with its glaring, dusty-looking banks, its vineyards and its ruins of castles, without variety of shade or distinct outline. On steaming slowly up, however, between Coblenz and Bingen, late on a summer evening, when the rocks are softened and blended, the vineyards almost lost, and the ruins stand out boldly against the summer sky, then the Rhine is indeed lovely. I am sure the Danube must be the same, but I did not feel at all sorry to go down to dinner amongst some of the most romantic scenery.

If there was nothing romantic in the dining-cabin, we had at least an excellent dinner, with plenty of vegetables and fruits. Opposite to me sat a most repulsive-looking old Hungarian. He reminded me very unpleasantly of an infirm old tiger I had once seen in some zoological gardens. As he took bones, flesh, and skin in his hands, glaring at the same time fiercely round, he munched them between his jaws. I am sure if any waiter had touched him, or offered to remove his plate, he would have growled. He was a horrid old man! His fork he only used when he stuck it into the dishes of compote or preserved fruits, very often missing his aim, and sometimes dropping one or two off his fork, which he put back with his hands into the dish. Alas! for the unwary traveller who ate compote or dried fruit next day! An old lady delighted me greatly by the innocent way with which, with silver grey hair, she wore a bright chestnut chignon! I hope she had them all colours, to suit the trimmings of her bonnet.

When about a couple of hours from Vienna, we took on board nearly a hundred cadets from a large military school. Some were going to a large military college in the Kaiserstadt, and others to another institution of the same kind near it. Most of them wore the Jäger uniform, the rest a cavalry dress. The amount of kissing that took place before they parted at their different destinations was wonderful.

The majority of them were mere boys, and they looked so very sorry to say good-bye. As they shook hands and kissed again and again, it seemed very simple and natural. But to us English it never can be anything but ludicrous to see a party of friends meet or part. The ladies bend coldly and distantly to the gentlemen; but the latter fall into each other's arms and embrace, hug, and kiss; and then kiss, hug, and embrace again and again, as if it would not be just as good to give a thoroughly hearty shake of the hands.

The fashion of kissing a lady's hand is still much used, and I think it a very pretty one, it seems so deferential and respectful, and yet so kindly. If any one you do not fancy offers to do so, you can always stop him without offence, by pretending you are thoroughly English, and shaking him heartily by the hand. He will be too astonished then to think of kissing, for ladies scarcely ever shake hands in Austria, though the custom is coming much more into fashion than formerly.

The water of the Danube does not allow the large steamers to go up to Vienna (and this year it was so low, that we had to land at a spot below the usual place). About half an hour, therefore, before reaching Vienna, two smaller steamers are generally waiting, into which passengers and luggage are hurried. In the suburbs of the city, and close to the river's bank, some marvellously handsome barracks are being built, in much too elaborate and costly a style of architecture for such a purpose. I heard murmurs from many on board at the lavish waste of so many millions of florins, when the country is so near bankruptcy as it is just now! I could not help mentally agreeing with the speakers, when I thought how much more usefully the money might have been employed.

Vienna is notoriously one of the most unhealthy cities of Europe, partly from its low situation, from the excessive dust, and from its very defective drainage. The obituary in most of the Vienna papers not only gives the names and ages of the deceased, but also the diseases of which they have died; and I noticed that, even this fine dry summer, more than half the deaths in Vienna were from lung diseases of various kinds. It is also a well-known fact that the Danube is a most insalubrious river, and, except Pressburg, every city through which it runs is more or less unhealthy. I suppose this arises from the inundations in winter, and from the quantity of light dust that is always blowing in summer, with the slightest breath of air, from the long reaches of sand-banks its waters leave when they recede. If it were not for the Danube they say that Pressburg would be the most healthy city in Europe.

Chapter IX.

BRUNN AM GEBERGE—SIGNAL FOR THE VILLAGE COWS—SENSELESS GAME—STATE OF RELIGION—PILGRIMAGES TO ST. MARIA ENZENSDORF—ABSURD CEREMONIES—ABUNDANCE OF FRUIT—IMPROVEMENTS IN AUSTRIAN INNS—SCHNELLSIEDER—PREPARATION OF COFFEE.

CHAPTER IX.

BRÜNN AM GEBERGE is a very small village, entirely surrounded by vineyards. A few people come out from Vienna for the summer months, and reside in some of the better class of houses and villas, of which there are only about half a dozen. Being so small, it cannot boast of a promenade or band, or any great attraction beyond its retirement, and, at the same time, its convenient proximity to Vienna. Its inhabitants seem to trade mostly in milk and butter; and the place swarms with cows.

At five o'clock every morning in summer, and at six o'clock in winter, a man goes the round of the village, playing different lively national tunes on a bugle. This is the signal for the cows to come out to pasture; and, accordingly, in every house you see a door thrown open, and animals of all sizes and colours make their appearance from the cottages; from some of them, two or three. They either saunter slowly or trot briskly down the streets to the spot where the cowherds are waiting for them. When they are all assembled, they are driven off to the field—not certainly to eat (as the pasture is generally meagre and poor), but perhaps for change of air and exercise, which may be considered good for them. They come home at eleven, decidedly more quickly than they set out. The cowherds have enormous leather whips, which, as they crack them round their heads with a report like that of a pistol, have a wonderful effect on the cows, seldom failing to bring any straggler up into the ranks. At twelve o'clock again the bugle is sounded, and once more the procession is formed, returning home at six o'clock—milking time. All is conducted so orderly and quietly. The cows come down the streets by themselves in such an exemplary manner, waiting patiently at the doors of their respective owners till they are let in. If kept waiting too long, they begin a gentle lowing, and sometimes a friendly passer-by opens the door for them.

Occasionally in the morning the maternal feelings of some cow gets the better of the dread of the crack of the heavy whip, and she turns round, instead of joining the herd, to take one more look in the home-shed, at the two or three days' old calf, which her instinct tells her will be sent to the butcher directly her back is turned. In this case, if the sound of the cracking leather thong is too far off to rouse her from her dream of affection, a baby three or four years old, clad in corduroy suit, is sent in charge of the beast, till it rejoins its companions.

One of the senseless games of a country where, alas! cricket is unknown, is for the herdsmen to assemble in a circle and try to outvie each other in cracking their whips! This is a harmless recreation, confined to saints' days and Sundays.

As far as I have discovered, cows and herdsmen are the only animals in Austria that really enjoy a rest on Sunday, as that is the only day the former are not taken out to pasture. Shops and exhibitions are open, and the advertisement sheet of the Vienna papers contains always a long list of theatres and balls, extra trains and other conveyances, especially for Sunday. The Jäger from the neighbouring barracks walk about in full-dress, and, with the fact that no cows are to be seen, their appearance makes the only difference I could discover between Sunday and week day. I must do the common people the justice to say that they never omit going to church once, if not twice, a day. Servants are equally observant of this duty. The absence of all religion in the middle classes, however, is something awful. There seems to be an utter want of all faith. No one appears to realize the ideas of immortality and eternity, and it is painful to hear these subjects discussed in this country. The hopeless idea that when we die we are no better off than the beasts that perish, is the creed which not only men but women openly profess. The mild and pure-minded Martin Luther cherished a bright and hopeful faith in a happy eternity, so comprehensive, that he would not even deny that dogs might have a hereafter; and his countrymen in the south now refuse to accept this glad solace for the miseries of life.

The adjoining village to Brünn is St. Maria Enzensdorf, a famous place for pilgrimages. In the early part of September several Hungarian processions came, headed by one or two bright banners. The men, who marched in two long lines, were dressed in the full white short trowsers, and loose white blouse, with open hanging sleeves and leather belt, which is the summer dress of the peasants in Hungary. These were followed by the women, dressed in cottons of every colour in the rainbow, orange and scarlet being principally predominant in the handkerchiefs which covered their heads. Every woman in the crowd carried on her back an enormous white bundle, which contained provisions for the road, and things to be blessed. These Hungarian pilgrims only came the first few days in September, and generally travelled by steamer to Vienna, whence they walked to the shrine. When they came within sight of St. Maria Enzensdorf, they broke forth into a loud chaunt, the men at the same time uncovering their heads, and showing their long sleek hair, parted down the middle, and hanging lank on each side of their whiskerless faces. They all looked so serious and so much in earnest that one could not help feeling sympathy and respect for them, sentiments very different from those with which one looked on the usual processions, which constantly passed, of men in chimney-pot hats and broadcloths, and of women in enormous crinolines, with tawdry bonnets or hats, covered with cheap gaudy artificial flowers, and carrying parasols of every imaginable hue, all whispering, chattering, and laughing together. As they moved on, the band played a merry polka, or Valkslied, or the crowd chaunted a hymn. In the middle of the latter I have seen a "chignoned" lady pursue a fat beadle, decked in gold lace and cocked hat, in order to hang a picture of St. Mary by a red tape round his neck. Such a mixture of religion and frivolity was never seen. It was the ignorance and superstition of the Dark Ages in the costume of the nineteenth century.

Inside the church the same disagreeable

feelings are forced on the mind, although there is very little of the cultivation of the present age wasted on its external or internal appearance as it is. The church is an ugly, uncared-for structure, the walls of which are covered with ostentatious votive offerings of pictures of every size and shape, some even large oil-paintings, containing a full-length likeness of the donor, and in some cases of the donors, with a sick child or an invalid parent—how correct the likeness, I cannot say—lying in bed. The presentation of these pictures surely betrays ignorance, vanity, and bad taste in those who can afford to make such expensive offerings. Even a mite given towards the embellishment of the house of God, to render it more worthy of the service for which it was intended, would be in better keeping with the feelings of gratitude and thankfulness for prayers answered and dear ones restored to health. The command not to let the right hand know what the left hand gives, would then be more implicitly obeyed than it is by thus placarding the holy walls with the names and addresses and likenesses of those who by so doing convert the house of God into a ludicrous representation of the booth of a travelling quack in a country fair!

It speaks very well for the honesty of the poor people who form these processions that, though they walk for weary miles along the hot dusty roads, with vineyards on each side, the grapes which hang so temptingly are never touched. The country all round abounds in fruit. Early in September we had delicious nectarines, small, but highly flavoured. Afterwards came a succession of peaches, also small, but very good. I did not appreciate the sort which they call

"Orangien," and in Italy "Non mi lasciar," the kernel of which grows into the fruit. The "Kernlöser" are very much better.

Such beautiful plates of fruit we used to have at all our meals!—dishes piled up with peaches, grapes, and nectarines, arranged with much taste with the natural leaves. The grapes are considered so wholesome that they are eaten rather freely. I never could make my kind Austrian host and hostess understand that a pound of grapes at each meal was more than we usually took in England. We also thought that eating them one at a time was more enjoyable than putting nearly a bunch into one's mouth at once.

One great comfort I enjoyed at Brünn was a bed long enough for me. It was the first I had had in which I could really sleep comfortably since I came to Germany. Sometimes, after a long day's walking, it was dreadful to squeeze oneself into a small box about five feet long—the length of almost all the bedsteads in the mountain inns. I was also glad to find that baths are not looked upon in Austrian houses as an unknown luxury, as is commonly supposed in England. In fact, railway-travelling, and intercourse with other nations, have been the means of introducing many excellent reforms into Austria, as they have into most countries.

Of course, in the very little towns off the beaten track, the inns are as destitute of comfort and convenience of any kind as they were in the first days of travelling, and you must expect to rough it in them. One great comfort in travelling is the possession of an Etna, or "Schnellsieder;" not a tea-kettle or tea-pot, as Mr. Murray advises, which would cause more trouble than comfort. A much more useful "Schnellsieder" may be bought in any town in Austria for seventy kreutzers than would be got in England for double that sum. "Spirituous" for burning may be purchased anywhere, and thus a cup of tea can be made in a few minutes. Besides, as the English are so dirty that they must be constantly washing, it is a comfort to be able to boil a little hot-water even in a friend's house, when kitchen-stoves are extinguished, and indulge in the luxury of a hand-washing when one fancies. Those who drink green tea had better bring it with them from England, as that which is bought while travelling is generally very coarse.

I wish, however, we in England would try to imitate the coffee which is made abroad, where it is as exceptional to get a bad cup as it is the reverse in England. One great fault we have in the process of preparing coffee is that of keeping it too long ready roasted and ground. Most families in Austria have a grand coffee roasting once a week, and it is only ground when it is wanted, or a certain portion for use daily. The following is an excellent receipt for coffee, from a soldier servant renowned for his skill in his concoction. A small table-spoonful of ground coffee is used for every cup wanted. When put into the coffee-pot it is pressed down very tight with the presser. When the presser is taken out, a very little water, *quite boiling*, is put into it, and it is closed up. When it is heard dripping a little more boiling water is added. When this has been repeated three times, the powder will be well saturated. Then fill up as much as you want, but always keep the water boiling; close the coffee-pot each time, and take out the tin rammer. Fresh roasted coffee should always be used. This method will never fail to make excellent clear strong coffee, without those eggshell or isinglass preparations which generally render it undrinkable.

Chapter X.

STREET SCENES IN BRUNN—HUNGARIAN OX-DRIVERS—CULTIVATION OF MAIZE—COUNTRY INNS—HERR AND FRAU VON H—— —EMPLOYMENT OF DOGS—PETERSDORF—BEAUTIFUL CHURCH—SUFFERINGS OF PETERSDORF FROM WAR—BESIEGED BY THE TURKS—JACOB TRINKGELD—DESTRUCTION OF THE HOSPITAL CHURCH.

CHAPTER X.

AT Brünn I felt sadly idle. I could have stood all day at the windows, and watched the ever-changing scene presented by the passers-by, so different from the wearisome promenade at Ischl, with its crowd of over-dressed women in rechauffé ball-dresses, its lounging officers and dandies, in their tedious treadmill movements up and down! At Brünn every moment there was something picturesque or unusual to arrest attention, and excite either wonder or amusement. A shrill, not unmusical cry of "Indianen," would call you to the window, and you would see pass by a large flock of turkeys, every shade of brown and white, driven by at least three dirty, picturesque-looking vagabonds, armed with long whips, with which they mercilessly flipped up any straying bird, keeping them in wonderful order. Repeating their cry of "Indianen," they stopped at every door in hope of customers.

These would be followed by several teams of the large pale grey Hungarian oxen, with their intelligent dark eyes, the mild expression of which contrasted so strangely with the fierce aspect of their enormous long horns, straight, curled, twisted, and drooping, in no two alike. Their drivers were no less interesting—all Hungarians, with their proud, erect bearing and reckless swagger, carrying their whips as if they were sceptres, and wearing their floating dirty white garments as if they were robes of royalty. They were very kind to their cattle, but kept aloof from their fellow-workers.

A group of dark, beautiful gipsy women would stop to count their gains, and see if they could afford money for tobacco at the small shop opposite. Such dark flashing Bohemian eyes, and black hair shining under the usual gaudy-coloured gipsy handkerchief! I used to be particularly amused watching a little peasant girl at the corner of the street, who had a small bench covered with fruit—ripe tempting clusters of grapes and plates of rosy-cheeked peaches, which she used to dispose of to the passers-by.

Though the grapes were only a kreutzer (not a farthing) a bunch, I often saw some tired, wandering harp-women, pale, sickly-looking children, or dusty carters, who had asked the price, turn away without purchasing any, because they found it too high for their limited purses. I felt really for them, but I consoled myself with the thought that further on in the neighbourhood they might find some cheaper, as every door nearly had its bench with saucers of fruit for sale.

Of the many picturesque figures I saw passing along the streets, I used to think some of the most striking in appearance were the women returning from the maize-fields, with their high baskets strapped to their shoulders, and loaded with the green maize drooping so gracefully, like waving green plumes, each broad leaf falling exactly where it ought, as if arranged by the hand of an artist. Maize is a most useful plant here, and there are many fields of it about Brünn, on the level grounds interspersed with the vineyards. They feed their cattle with the fresh cut green leaves.

When dry, they stuff their mattresses with them, and the grain is the principal food of their poultry; but I doubt it is not distributed to them with a very open hand, for never in Austria, except at private houses, have I eaten poultry which could possibly have partaken—at least, in sufficient quantity—of anything so nourishing as Indian corn.

I would strongly advise all travellers in Austria for *once* carefully to avoid good Mr. Murray's advice in his useful hand-book, and never order " gebackenes Huhn," unless they are so accommodating as to be able to dine contentedly on bones and batter. We have generally found, at most country inns, the veal cutlets, which are always ready, very good. At some mountain inns they smile at the idea of meat; but then you have the acceptable alternative of fresh-caught trout, smoking-hot plain-boiled potatoes, and excellent butter. One hint I would offer is, always (if you can) to dine as near one o'clock as possible, if you wish for soup—before one is best, and not after. The rule is, "First come, first served;" and those who arrive late have only the remains of the soup first served, filled up with boiling water—horribly weak stuff, and always reminding me of a third cup of tea!

I must now return from my long digression, and again take my idle seat at the window. I must do myself, however, the justice to say I always had a bit of work in hand, though the progress it made was marvellously slow. I consoled myself, however, with the reflection that, when one is out for a holiday, one has a right to be idle.

There was one object that passed on which I always gazed with much awe and wonder. This was an old paralytic man, drawn in a bath-chair. He was enormously rich—the Marquis of Carabbas of the place. At least, his wife was Marchioness of Carabbas, as the old gentleman himself had sunk to the condition of a nonentity since his illness. Every house you stopped to admire in the village belonged to the Frau von H——. A beautifully-cultivated kitchen-garden we passed was Frau von H——'s. A large herd of cows which went past, or several teams of horses, which we admired as they were led or driven along the street, were all Frau von H——'s. The blacksmith's forge, the carpenter's shop, the butcher's stall, the vineyards, the maize fields, all—all were hers; until at last I came to the conclusion that if there was anything that did not belong to Frau von H——, it could only be the church and the railway.

The old man was said to be very hard and cruel. A boy in his service had once so excited his rage that he beat him with such severity that he died in consequence. Herr von H——, according to the village legend, only escaped just punishment by paying a very large sum to the officers of justice; in addition to which he was condemned constantly to wear a black rope round his neck, which the public executioner from Vienna comes once a month to inspect, supplying a new one when wanted.

Very different were the feelings with which I regarded the poor dogs in this place; which, though kindly treated, are much used here as beasts of burden, especially for dragging grinding organs, which abound in this town, three or four playing before my windows every morning, and often two grinding at the same time a "Czardas," and "God save the Emperor." Luckily for the dogs, a tax has just been put on them; and as their labours may consequently be dispensed with, probably their days of hard work are over.

About half an hour's walk from Brünn, on the road towards Rodaun, at the foot of some hills, lies the small town of Perchtoldsdorf, commonly called Petersdorf. It is a very small place, but has a beautiful church, and some interesting remains of an ancient castle. The church is considered a "beautiful monument of powerful Gothic architecture." It is built over a small underground church, which is supposed to have been erected in the time of the Knights

Templars, in the reign of Leopold the Glorious, 1208—1209.

The beautiful upper church seems to have been used for a magazine till the year 1420, when the good Princess Beatrice, widow of Prince Albert the Fourth, restored it, and dedicated it to St. Elizabeth. She also founded an hospital for poor people and pilgrims. The beautiful church-tower stands alone, about twenty feet from the east end of the building. The lower part was formerly a chapel, dedicated to St. Nicholas. The altar-stone is still to be seen, and in the centre is a trap-door, through which is a draw-well, to be used in case of a siege. The ascent to the top is nearly two hundred feet, and a fine view is obtained from it towards the Styrian mountains. In the tower hang seven bells, and every day at three o'clock three bells are chimed, a custom the origin of which tradition assigns to the Knights Templars.

The church, which, with the tower, is built of freestone, is a beautiful building, with very high slender Gothic pillars, a fine high altar, and six side ones. In its palmy days it must have been a magnificent and impressive edifice; but troubles seem to have fallen thick and fast on Petersdorf from an early time. Hardly were the Castle and walls finished, the church restored, and the hospital built, when the Hungarians, under John Hunyad, plundered the town, and set it on fire. It was soon after restored and rebuilt. Civil wars afterwards broke out, and Petersdorf was constantly the theatre of fighting and tumult. In 1463 it was pledged to Counts von Pöfing and St. George. In consequence of a diversity of misfortunes it became a mere ruin till

1521, when the walls were strengthened and rebuilt, and the tower was restored. Three years later the Rath-haus and St. Leonhard's church were also repaired. Those works were not done too soon, for eight years after came a powerful Turkish host, which surrounded the walls; but only the hospital, church, and the houses outside the town, fell into the hands of these invaders. A long peace then followed, till the year 1605, when the Hungarian rebels, under Bocskay, marched to the walls of Petersdorf, and burnt the hospital and church.

More dreadful was the fate of the town in 1683. Light troops of Spahis and Tartars showed themselves on the 9th of July before its walls. The armed burghers at first drew back, but on the 10th and 12th of the some month sallies were unsuccessfully made. We have a record of the siege by the town magistrate, Jacob Trinkgeld.

When the Turkish army of 200,000 men raised the siege of Raab, the roving Tartars and rebels were ordered to scour the whole land of Austria south of the Danube, and lay it waste with fire and sword. They fought with such fury against Petersdorf that it was impossible to resist them; and when, their powder getting low, they proceeded to burn the town in several places, the besieged thought it best to remove their goods and property, and withdraw into the church, which was considered fire-proof. Their wives and children were placed, for greater safety, in the small under-ground church.

On the 18th, after the town had been burnt, a Turk, waving a white flag, came down the High Street, and proceeded to dictate terms to the besieged. They were summoned to do homage to the conqueror, and pay a ransom of 4,000 florins, on compliance with which terms they might come forth from the church and tower, and their lives would be secure. The next morning the Pasha came from Vienna with a large force, and for five hours he sat on a red carpet awaiting the reply of the besieged. After serious consultation, the men resolved to yield, and as they came forth from the church, their arms were taken from them, the Turks saying those who did homage did not require weapons. When they were in the market-place, and after they had been examined by fifty Turks, to see whether they had any gold concealed about their persons, they were all, by a barbarous order of the Pasha, murdered. According to the old chronicle, " This blood-ball lasted from one o'clock till two. Only two escaped. One concealed himself in the clock of the tower, and the other in the well under St. Leonard's Tower." In the underground church they still show the hole that was broken in the strong iron-bound door in order to bring out the unhappy wives and children, who were all sent into slavery. Three thousand five hundred heads were sent to Vienna, and after being exposed in the market-place, were thrown into one grave.

When peace was again restored, the bones of the unfortunate men were collected, and buried at Petersdorf, where, on the old church walls, is a tablet with the inscription, " Here rest in peace, from the slaughter of the Turks, 3,500 burghers and neighbours. God give them everlasting peace!" Yearly, on the 19th of July, a requiem of remembrance is chanted in Petersdorf Church for the rest of the souls of the slain. In the Town-hall is a series of pictures, executed in 1700, representing the whole scene of carnage, the record of the before-mentioned Jacob Trinkgeld being attached.

In 1703, some Styrian colonists settled in Petersdorf, and houses sprang up, and, except for the visit of the plague in 1713, peace and comfort seemed to have settled down at last on this devoted little town. In the Town-hall there is a very queer clock, fixed in the trunk of a tree, which, with its branches lopped off about half a foot from the stem, and polished, makes the clock-case. A Turkish Pasha is said to have been hanged on this tree, a legend which is still fondly cherished; for to the poor beleaguered inhabitants such a capture and punishment were events to be kept in remembrance. Since we left Brünn, we have heard with regret that the hospital, church, and several houses near have again been burnt down. Poor Petersdorf must be a doomed town!

Chapter XI.

GERMAN VINEYARDS—THE TRADE IN GRAPES—AUSTRIAN WINES—STRAW WINE—GROWTH OF MAIZE—THE MARQUIS OF CARABBAS—THE VINTAGE—ROMANCE AND REALITY—A VINTAGE SUPPER.

CHAPTER XI.

WHEN I first arrived at Brünn I was constantly awakened during the night by guns fired in all directions. I was informed it was the watchers in the vineyards keeping away thieves, but was afterwards assured that the watchers themselves steal many more grapes than the thieves.

There is a certain charm about the name of vineyards and vintage, which sounds well in poetry, and really exists in Italy, but certainly in Germany and Austria has no existence. The vines are just as stunted about here as they are on the Rhine, and at the end of every autumn are cut down close to the ground. From this knobby stump spring the year's shoots, which seldom grow higher than four feet, and are tied at two or three intervals with wisps of straw to strong short poles. The grapes grow on the young shoots, but quite close to the old trunk of the vine, so that they hang within half a foot of the ground. I suppose they ripen more quickly being so close to the hot earth, but they also come in for a good share of dust and mud. Looking at a fine garden in September, when the leaves begin to colour, one would say the tints are beautiful, but a field of waving corn is infinitely prettier and more graceful.

Like the cherries in West Kent, the produce of the vines is most frequently bought at an early stage of their growth by some rich speculator, who generally buys the produce of the whole district round. From him, for a very trifling sum, one may purchase the privilege of walking through the vineyards at any time. Otherwise every short cut and every cross-road is forbidden during the grape season, when we must keep to the public roads and wagon-tracks.

It is not always worth while, however, purchasing this privilege, for after walking some distance through a vineyard, we often come to a door that is locked, and have to retrace our steps.

This year the vintage is magnificent, and both here and in Hungary there has not been such a season for years. Grapes are selling for fourpence a gallon. We get a mixture of all sorts—some small as currants, and not much worth eating, others with a delicious muscadel flavour—large purple, large white, thick skins and thin skins. Some we cannot eat without staining the tips of our fingers a bronzy red hue. These are called squinting grapes. They told me that they were going to try and grow the true muscadel grape; but very seldom is there such a wonderfully good year for grapes as the present (1868) has been. The winters also are bitterly cold and long, so that I should fear the experiment of introducing the more delicate sorts of grapes would not answer. However, at present, the different sorts grow pretty much mixed together in the vineyards; and if a few white vines grow among the red, they are not particular in sorting them separately, but throw them all together into the mash-tub.

As a general rule, the purple grapes of all sorts are made into the red, and the different flavoured white grapes into the white *vin ordinaire*. Both sorts are sold for thirty kreutzers a bottle. The white wine is very agreeable and pleasant in hot weather, though rather sharp and very weak. The red wine is the nicest I have tasted in Austria, and has a most peculiar Russia leather flavour, almost like that of dry sherry. When it is of genuine quality, it is found also to have more body than the white. It is not the least like Vöslau, though grown so near, and they call it simply *vin ordinaire*.

They have a more costly sort, which they think much of, though it is called "straw wine." The grapes are selected and laid carefully on straw for a month, till they are nearly as dry as raisins. The wine which is then produced from them is very luscious, like Malaga, with a slight flavour of straw! This variety is thought so precious that it is only taken in small liqueur glasses, or, as they are elegantly called here, Schnapps-gläser.

The first days of the vintage are heralded by the appearance of full-filled waggons and barrows of green boughs which pour into the town. If we follow these to their destinations, we find that in almost all the court-yards, or little back-yards, even of the poorest houses, they use them to construct bowers or arbours of green boughs. At many houses a pole, with a green bough swinging from it, is hoisted from a window, or a gateway, as a sign that "wine is sold here, to be drunk on the premises." The wine which is thus retailed, is the refuse and odds and ends of casks of last year's vintage, and it is consumed so copiously that the whole population is more or less drunk. The wine is such weak stuff, a sour inky compound, that the quantity they must imbibe before it takes effect must be marvellous.

Gradually the boughs disappear one by one as the wine is consumed; and then begins a general cleaning out, when the whole place smells from morning till night of wine dregs and old casks. In such circumstances the atmosphere is anything but agreeable, especially in the very hot weather.

The vintage did not commence till the last week in September. We received a fortnight's notice of it, and an invitation to join the first picking party. About the middle of the month we were told that the grapes for the table were getting very scarce, an announcement which caused us some surprise, as the village was surrounded by vineyards, and the grapes were hanging thick and ripe on every side. However, the statement was explained by the fact that in Austria every measure of wine that is made pays a tax to the Government. When the grapes are fully ripe, therefore, they are forbidden to be cut, as any diminution of the quantity of wine would lower the amount of the tax.

The maize that is cut green for the cattle is grown amongst the vines. When the peasants go with their large baskets to fill them with this grain, they generally cut some grapes also, which they hide at the bottom. By this dishonest little trick, grapes are always to be had. The law cannot be very strict, or the grapes would not be openly sold at every corner of the streets.

At last came the day I had eagerly anticipated, when I should for the first time join the "vintage throng." When the heat of the day was over, we proceeded through forbidden paths and closed vine-clad alleys to the scene of harvest, which certainly

fell far short of that described by poets.
At the entrance to the vineyard, in a piece
of waste land, were vats and barrels.
Horses, decorated with flowers and hung
with bells, were the only objects that had
anything romantic or poetical in their appearance. Men from the vintage ground
kept bringing in baskets full of beautiful
purple grapes, which were thrown in clusters, just as they were picked, on a wire
tray, stretched over a large wooden tub.
Two men, standing on each side, with
their *hands* rubbed and squeezed the juice
of the grapes through the fine wire-work.
I wondered if this explained how the wine
acquired that pleasant dry flavour which
it has. In Italy they do it with their feet.
I prefer, however, the Austrian plan. When
enough had been pressed, the juice was
poured into a barrel, which was hoisted

on the decorated cart and drawn home, there to go through the process of fermentation, &c. Much of it must have been wasted, as the ground round was saturated with juice, spilled in consequence of the clumsy way in which it is handled.

I must not forget to notice that the Marquis of Carabbas was seated here; and before I left Brünn, I came to the conclusion that he was a much-maligned character. He really was of a remarkably hospitable, genial nature, very appreciative of a joke and of fun; and when he threw back his head for a hearty laugh, I looked in vain for any traces of the mark of the black rope under his neck.

When we joined the workers in the vineyard, we found the vines so closely planted together, that it was very difficult to walk between the rows, even in these days of reduced crinoline. A few years ago we must have looked on from a distance.

The vineyard consisted of about eight acres, and it was all to be picked before night. About twenty or thirty men and women were hard at work; but the scene is not to compare with that of hop-picking. The grapes grow so close to the ground, that the pickers have generally to stoop, so that they are hidden from view—a position which is very fatiguing. The grapes also stain the hands nearly as much as the hops; and some are extremely dusty and muddy. When I demurred against throwing some dirty ones into the baskets, the men said it was all the same—the juice would come out clean enough. We picked on till night came on, and it was so dark, one could not tell leaves from grapes.

Some of the bunches were splendid, weighing, I am sure, three quarters of a pound. In many the dried tendrils and small green leaves had grown tightly wedged in amongst the thick growing bunches, and looked so pretty that I often had to stop in my picking to admire them. The peasants, too, quite appreciated the beauty of the fruit, and often called my attention to a particularly fine cluster.

At last work was over, and the order came to leave. Before returning with the others I took one look at the moonlight scene. The situation of the vineyard, on a sloping hill, with a rivulet at the foot, was very picturesque. On every side rose hills clad with vines, their foliage fast turning scarlet under the hot rays of a long summer. Before us we could see, far away across the Danube, plains extending to Hungary, while on the right stood out the ruins of the Castles of Babenberg and Liechtenstein. A glorious harvest-moon shone out bright and clear. As the only English person present, I had been considerate enough not to wear any of the modern unpoetic adornments of the day, and even my bonnet hung on my arm.

As we wended our way slowly in single file through the narrow vineyard paths towards Brünn, I could not help thinking how very far the scene, beautiful as it was, fell short of those pictures of the vintage by which painters and poets have taught us to form exaggerated ideas of its glory and charm. The peasants were much too busy when picking to think of singing the "vintage chorus," and when work was over they were much too tired. The only vintage songs I heard were in the late hours of the night, and were sung in very uncertain melody, and in remarkably falsetto voices. The most cheerful sound heard during the vintage is the merry jingle of the horses' bells as they trot backwards and forwards from the farms to the vineyards with the large casks of wine-juice.

If we could have staid, however, to be present at the vintage supper, I believe we should have seen something realizing more completely our ideas of the vintage. The tables groan under huge masses of meat and heavy dumplings. The feast is so abundant that one has an opportunity of seeing what German appetites can compass. There is also an unbounded supply of new wine. Dancing concludes the entertainment, and, as may be easily imagined, the mirth by the morning gets fast and furious. A band is soon found amongst these people, as wandering harpers, principally women, abound. The Zither, or Cither, is a favourite instrument, and you rarely pass a wine-house, or "restauration," without hearing one of them, sometimes accompanied by the voice.

Chapter XII.

DAY AT LAXENBURG—HOUSE OF CORRECTION FOR WOMEN—
COUNT CHORINSKY AND JULIE EBERGENYE—INSTITUTION
FOR DEACONESSES—PALACE AND GARDENS—CASTLE OF
FRANZENBERG—MÖDLING—CASTLE OF LIECHTENSTEIN—
CHURCH OF ST. OTHMAR.

CHAPTER XII.

ONE bright sunny day we spent at Laxenburg. It was as hot as June, and delightfully pleasant under the splendid trees, and amongst the sweet-smelling flower-beds of the park.

On the way from Brünn, about a mile from the road, we passed a group of white buildings, clustered round a large white-washed edifice, which stood prominently forward, for miles an ugly and unsightly object in this uninteresting flat country. This is the Neudorf House of Correction for women; and here the wretched Julie Ebergenye is consigned to work out her twenty years of imprisonment.

Her partner in crime, Count Chorinsky, is undergoing the same sentence in the prison at Passau, on the Danube.

The story of their crime, its swift discovery, and their subsequent trial was in all the English papers early in the spring of this year. Owing to the rank and position of the criminals, it made a very painful sensation in Austria. The story in detail is too horrible to relate, but a slight summary may be briefly given.

I must first explain that in Austria there is an institution of deaconesses, into which, if a young lady can trace an unbroken ancestry for sixteen generations, she is admitted. They have apartments provided for them, as well as an addition to any income they possess. In Vienna they have six hundred florins yearly; in Prague, in the Hradschin, one thousand florins; in the Neustadt "Stift," one thousand florins; and in Brünn, nine hundred florins.

Their only duty is to attend mass daily. They sleep in their room when in residence, which is compulsory for the whole of the first year. At Neustadt their food is provided as at a mess, and they pay very little. They have also an opera-box. A carriage and footman is shared between every two or three. They have the independence and privileges of married women when in society. The institution was originally almost a religious foundation, and generally only old ladies were appointed. It is said that the Emperor Joseph, on some young lady being proposed, said, "Oh! she is not ugly enough yet!"

Shielded by these privileges, Julie Ebergenye seems to have rushed headlong into that life of vice and dissipation which is so common in Vienna. At last her roving affections fixed themselves on Count Chorinsky, but a bar to their happiness was the paramount obstruction of a wife. This nobleman had, years ago, married a public singer, and of this marriage he had long grown weary. The wife also was unhappy, wearied perhaps of his society, or it might be of the neglect with which he treated her, and had been for some time living a not very creditable life in Munich. Her death, however, was soon resolved on; and, as a first step, Julie Ebergenye went to Munich, and *accidentally* made the acquaintance of the Countess. Congenial spirits, they soon became apparently fast friends.

One evening, Julie Ebergenye, on her way to the Opera, called on the Countess, and took tea with her. In a short time she came out of the sitting-room, and begged the servant of the Countess Chorinsky to order her a carriage. When the carriage arrived, the servant went up to announce it; but the saloon door was closed and locked. The servant imagined that the ladies had got tired of waiting, and gone to the Opera on foot.

Next morning, as the door was still fast, it was determined to break it open. When this was done, the dead body of the wretched Countess Chorinsky was found. As the key of the door and the tea-pot were missing, this, with the disappearance of Julie Ebergenye, gave sufficient clue to the police. With the strange fatality which so often accompanies crime, Julie Ebergenye had carried with her the tea-pot containing the dregs of the poison, and also the key of the room in which the murder was committed. A full clue was discovered in a packet of Count Chorinsky's letters, found on the female prisoner, many of them urging her on to the commission of the frightful crime, " for which Heaven would bless her!"

The means employed in the accomplishment of the crime were clearly disclosed at the trial. From the deposition of the landlady of the house in which Countess Chorinsky lodged, it appeared that the unfortunate woman was urged to go to her and borrow some opera-glasses. During her absence, it was inferred, her " friend" took the opportunity of putting the poison into the tea-pot. There can be no doubt the crime was clearly proved, and the prisoners were sentenced to twenty years imprisonment with hard labour. This sentence seems a light one for such a crime, but everyone who considers what twenty years in the prison of Neudorf must be, cannot but conclude that death would be the more desirable punishment.

What can be more dreary than the life of the female prisoner? She sits in a large room, engaged in spinning, clad in the dark coarse prison dress, and with her hair cut close. Strict silence is enforced by the warders in attendance; but as there are women of all classes, some of them the lowest dregs of humanity, even the presence of the turnkeys at times does not prevent scenes of fearful violence, when they spring at each other like wild beasts, and can only be separated by seizing them by the throats and half strangling them! How miserable must such an existence be to a young woman of six-and-twenty, accustomed to all the refinements and luxuries of life! Fancy how dull must be the long, wearisome summer days, with their tedious and monotonous task! How dreary must be the long winter nights, when the winds howl dismally round the prison walls, as if reproaching her for the crimes which have made her the inmate of a gaol. What must be her reflections during the week spent in solitary confinement at each anniversary of her crime, in that gloomy November, when the fogs, creeping up from the Danube, wrap the prison, as it were, in a shroud. If she can over-live these twenty years, what will be her feelings when she leaves those walls, and returns amongst her fellow-men, stripped of honours and position, and with the never-dying memory of her crime.

Laxenburg, the present palace, and the old building which stands close by, do not contain anything to interest the visitor. The Imperial servants, however, were most anxious to show us the rooms occupied by Prince Napoleon, which on inquiry proved to be those recently done up, and inhabited, during a two days' stay this summer, by Prince Jerome Bonaparte. As, however, their inspection did not possess any attraction for us, we declined, and proceeded at once, and alone, to admire the beautiful trees which surrounded the palace, many of them of great age and large girth.

The flower-beds on the lawn were most tastefully laid out in ribbon patterns, not too complicated or artificial-looking. The bright hot summers in this part of Austria soon give a very tropical appearance to the gardens that are really cared for. Most of the hot-house plants are turned out in May into the open borders, and by constant care and watering they soon attain, under the hot bright sun, a luxuriant growth which, alas! in England they never acquire.

The oak-trees are very fine, and some of them of a great age. They abound in squirrels—"oak-cats," as they call them here. I must confess there are rather too many statues and bridges. "Knight's shrines," "Farms," "Hero monuments," and such ornamental structures, surprise one too frequently. The trees, however, are so thick and luxuriant that all these little Cockney edifices do not burst on us at once, and we have time, in admiring the glories of nature, to recover from the effects produced by art.

At the end of the park, in a temple erected on an island in the lake, is a most perfect specimen of ancient Roman mosaic, in excellent preservation. The floor of the principal saloon, I should think eighteen or twenty feet square, is entirely composed of it. In the centre are two figures, "Theseus and Ariadne." It was brought from Salzburg, where it was accidentally discovered when they were digging in Mozart's Platz for a foundation for the statue erected in honour of that composer, in 1842.

On the largest island in the lake is built in red stone an exact representation of an ancient castle in the time of the Templars. The approach to it is by a heavy ferry-boat, worked by windlass; but I should certainly strike work if I were the ferry-woman, for the work must be both tedious and hard. In the interior are most lovely gems of ancient Venetian glass, old china, jewelled reliques, beautiful old china stones, old silver, and crystal goblets. Of all it contains, however, some of the ceilings are the objects that most took my fancy. They are of oak and other woods, so beautifully carved, many of them hundreds of years old, taken from old castles in the Tyrol, or in Upper Austria. One is especially striking, with very massive and rich carving, and inlaid with heavy bosses of steel; it came from Wallenstein's house at Eger in Bohemia.

The chapel is extremely small, and built exactly after one at Kloster Neuburg, which Leopold the Glorious built; and the altar is from a small parish church in Styria, the first Christian church built in those parts. In short, churches, castles, and houses seem to have been ransacked for treasures to decorate this toy castle. The vestry of the chapel contains the holy vessel which held the sacrament with which the priest gave the benediction to the Emperor Maximilian the First, when he was hanging suspended from the edge of a precipice which he had ventured too near in the ardour of chamois-hunting in the Tyrol. He was luckily rescued by a mountaineer, on a poaching expedition, who came to his assistance.

In a room adjoining the chapel, is a large oil-painting representing the rescue of the Emperor; but there has been more than a painter's licence allowed in the representation, as the Emperor is kneeling in great comfort in a very snug little cave on the face of the precipice. The rest of the hunt and a mass of people are below, with the priest and attendants.

The castle also contains a dungeon and a torture-chamber. A fine view is seen from the summit of the watch-tower—at least, as good a view as can be expected in this hopelessly flat country. We see as far as Vienna on one side—to the Schneeberg and Styrian hills on the south. The rising grounds above Brühl are visible in the west; and our gaze may wander far away over the long flat plain of Hungary on the east.

After the ascent of the tower, we have seen all the sights of the Castle of Franzensberg, and can again wander out into the park and enjoy the shade of the beautiful trees, or explore numberless walks, and discover cascades, rustic bridges, fish-ponds, and temples at every turn. Near the castle is a tilting-yard, one hundred and fifty-four paces long, and seventy-seven wide, where occasionally tournament parties are held. After that is seen, we have finished the tour of Laxenburg, and have only to stroll about the lovely grounds, or drink coffee or beer at the "Goldener Stern," which is close to the royal palace, till it is time to return.

On the way between Laxenburg and Brünn, we pass through the very interesting town of Mödling, where also a day can be very pleasantly spent in exploring the Rathhaus, the curious remains of the old parish church, and the very picturesque church of St. Othmar (which makes a beautiful sketch from the barracks). The town itself is full of picturesque houses and streets. The Rathhaus is a queer, picturesque-looking building, and in front is a drinking-fountain, from the centre of which grows a tree, with long graceful plumes of coarse grass round the roots— it is so pretty!

From Mödling a lovely walk under fine stone pines takes us up the valley of the Brühl, and over its vineclad hills, past five or six ruins of old castles, some of them flagrantly artificial. Among them, however, are the real remains of the Liechtenstein and Babenberg strongholds. They must have been grand-looking residences before the sixteenth and seventeenth centuries, when the wild Turkish hordes poured themselves over the land, laying everything waste before them with fire and sword. Prince Liechtenstein has built himself an exceedingly comfortable-looking, good-sized modern house, from which he looks, no doubt without regret, over the smooth lawns and beautifully-arranged flower-beds, at the old ruined homes of his ancestors.

With the churches about here it is different. No one has cared to restore them, and until recently they were in a sad state. The Church of St. Othmar, after standing unroofed for more than a hundred years, has at last been roofed, cleaned whitewashed, painted, and covered with gilding.

Some of the remains are of exquisite beauty, such as the fragments of fine columns and delicate, graceful stonework. There is also a remnant of a finely-carved Sacramentshäuslein, with exceedingly curious wrought open-work iron doors, impossible to describe. It is very ingeniously constructed, and, we were informed, drew forth high commendations from a connoisseur in antiquities. There is also here, as at Petersdorf, an under-church, now only used as a wood or store-house; and in the churchyard stands the tower, with a cupola-shaped, mosque-like wooden top; but it is not very large or high. St. Othmar is supposed to have been built by the Knight Templars.

Chapter XIII.

RAILWAY FROM VIENNA TO LINZ—VIEWS ROUND SALZBURG—CAVES OF THE UNTERSBERG—THE SLEEPING WARRIORS OF KAISER KARL—GNOMES—A PROPHETIC TREE—STRIFE IN A CONVENT—APPEARANCE AND COSTUME OF THE PEASANTRY—DIALECT OF THE DISTRICT.

CHAPTER XIII.

WE could not stay long enough in Brünn to attend the vintage feast, as the harvest would occupy three weeks longer, and we had to go to Salzburg. So we bade adieu to the happy vintage grounds, and all the glories and delights of Vienna, and found ourselves, without adventure or incident, safely arrived at Salzburg.

The railway from Vienna to Linz is nearly equal to the journey by Danube steamer between those cities. The course which it takes is winding and pretty. It is very pleasant when, after passing

Linz, we come in sight of the beautiful ranges of mountains again; though all tastes do not agree even about mountains. One of the servants was gazing wistfully from the railway platform at Brünn over the flat, dreary plains which stretched for miles around, only varied by herds of cattle and a line of dust-clouds which marked the high road from Vienna.

"It is very ugly," remarked her mistress.

"Oh! dear no," said the servant, who was a Highlander. "I was thinking how very beautiful such very even, flat land is. I am so tired of mountains—I have seen them all my life."

What we are accustomed to, we do not often value; and as frequently we set an undue worth on what is scarce or uncommon. Some years ago, we were travelling in North Italy, on our way home from Malta, and we had a Maltese servant with us. One night we stopped at an inn to sleep, before the ascent of the Simplon.

Strolling out in the evening, we came upon the Maltese leaning over a bridge which crossed a broad mountain stream. The noise of the rushing water prevented the man hearing us till we came quite close, and we saw he was gazing most wistfully into the waters. On being asked if the stream was not very beautiful, he answered,

"Oh! most beautiful! but it makes me sad to see such good water running away, and all wasted."

He had been comparing this mighty stream with the tiny rills which are thought so precious, and guarded so jealously, in his sunny but arid little island.

This summer some foreigners were visiting in Salzburg, and expressed great disappointment with the place. "How could people talk of the beautiful scenery? Why, the mountains shut out all the view." Perhaps they also would have preferred the "beautiful even plains."

I cannot understand anyone being disappointed in the scenery round Salzburg. There are miles of rich fertile pasture lands, sufficiently varied with fine avenues and orchards of fruit-trees to make the rides and drives for a great distance round sheltered and pleasant; while in the distance we behold chains of the most beautifully-broken and rugged mountains. Nearer the city, the mighty Untersberg rears itself to a height of six thousand feet. In its rich caverns the Kaiser Karl, with his hosts of armed men, is sunk in a magic sleep—

Emperor, knights, and soldiers, all repose with their arms in their hands, waiting till the Emperor's beard shall have grown three times round a table at which he is seated. His daughter Emma, whose duty it is to measure this beard, is near. When the magnificent beard has for the third time made the circumference of the table, this powerful host, roused from the magic spell of sleep, will start to their arms, and will make their war-cry ring through the caves and vaults of Untersberg. A fearful battle, according to popular prophecy, is then to rage on the fertile plains below; after which Germany is once more to form a united empire! How those stern old warriors must have stirred in their sleep, impatient at the slow growth of their Emperor's beard, when the Prussian armies swept through the fatherland! No doubt when the fulness of the time is accomplished, they will know how to unite Germany under one imperial sceptre by the flash of their bright swords and the power of their strong arms.

These sleeping warriors are waited on by gnomes, queer little brown men, not many inches high, whose resemblance is carved in wood by most of the woodworkers around. They are perfectly harmless and inoffensive, and inclined to be kind to the peasants; but since the times of railways and tourists they are not often seen. On three or four days in the year, at midnight, they congregate in the Cathedral, and at a few other churches, where they hold high mass. Such are the legends, firmly believed by the peasants, of the marvels contained in the Untersberg or Wunderberg.

The house that my friends have just purchased here is a most charming little nest, perched up on a ledge of rock on the Nonnberg, with just room for a carriage to creep up to the door. Behind the house the beautiful rocks rise steep up to the Castle. So bluff and precipitous are they, that when the snow melts, or a heavy rain falls, a wooden covered sluice, which runs along the back of the house, is opened, and the water is carried off under the house. If this is neglected most disastrous results follow, and the water has been known to pour in through ceilings, wardrobes, and stones.

The view from these windows is most lovely, over the rich, fertile plains, where the peasants are now (in October) busily employed getting in a *third* and very good-looking crop of hay. In the middle distance rise the hills round Hellbrünn, with their rich covering of trees in their autumnal hues; while further off is a panorama of wonderful beauty, in the high chains of the Noric Alps. Just below our feet lie gardens and orchards, with a few houses among them. In their midst the parish church stands up very prominently.

The vines have even here been covered with an abundant crop of splendid grapes. The climate is generally so cold that they do not ripen every summer, but this hot season has produced a marvellous show. Apples and pears, too, have been abundant.

The most remarkable wonder near Salzburg is a magic pear-tree, that grows near the Untersberg. When this tree blossoms it is believed to be a sure foreboding of war. In 1848 it was covered with bloom, and again in 1866, when crowds went out from Salzburg to see it.

We are in very good company here, for, besides having the church just below us, we have also a convent close by, with a chapel containing some curious paintings round the altar. The closely-trellised galleries, where the nuns sit, look very mysterious. Who that sees the calm, serene expression of their faces would imagine that even in such a place worldly thoughts and worldly strifes intrude? I fear there is but too much reason to believe so.

An Austrian friend of mine was quartered in Bergamo. From the citadel the officers looked down upon the town, and amongst other places a convent garden, where they used often to see the nuns walking. In fine weather it was usual for them to carry out their work and employ themselves at their needle. The officers noticed that at one time they suddenly divided themselves into separate parties, which always avoided any communication with each other. One day, however, a fearful commotion was observed amongst the gentle devotees. They rushed about in all directions, with abundant gesticulation. What was it that had so suddenly roused them from their usual lethargy into such a state of excitement?

A few days afterwards the officers learned from a lady in the town the solution of the mystery. A German archbishop in Bergamo had just died, and a young Italian was appointed as his successor. The nuns separated into two parties, one remaining faithful to the old love, and the other eager to throw itself into the arms of the new. One side were all for the excellent deceased, and the other were for the expected Italian. The war of words between the fair opponents ran at last so high, that, in a fit of pious zeal, one of the nuns stabbed another with her scissors. The wound was a severe one, and unfortunately ultimately proved fatal. And this act of violence was perpetrated in the calm retirement of convent life!

Salzburg is so close to the Bavarian frontier, that many of the peasant women of that country come in on market or saint days. They wear the frightful high, black-glazed hat of Bavaria, contrasting unfavourably with the head-dress of the women of the Salzkammergut, which is very pretty and useful. It consists only of a square of black silk tied tightly round the head, drawn in folds behind, and the ends left hanging on each side. For full dress they also wear a black velvet bodice, ornamented with silver buttons, and a broad necklace, composed of seven or eight chains of silver, fastened in front by a deep-embossed or jewelled clasp, and worn tight round the neck. This ornament is worn in a great measure to conceal the large goitres and full throats which abound in this town.

The women are singularly plain in Salzburg. Even their own countryman, in his guide-book, says he must be ungallant enough to mention that they "are small, and possess little beauty!" Nor have the men anything to boast of, for in their own way they are no better-looking than the women; and people ascribe their inferior looks very much to the way in which they spend their lives. Remaining in close rooms, heated by stoves, the whole or greater part of the day, and breathing only the stifling fumes of tobacco smoke, or what Herr Noë calls "*mephistischen Dünsten*," can be favourable neither to the production of beauty nor to the development of muscular strength.

The peasant men are quite as fond of silver ornaments as the women. They wear broad, pointed velvet waist-bands, generally embroidered in silver, with some select motto or expressive word. Their coats too are covered with rows of either plain silver buttons, or silver groschen made into buttons. For its size, there are almost as many silver shops in Salzburg as in Genoa; and the things are not at all dear, provided you get a German to buy them for you; for though the shopkeepers in Salzburg are not quite so hostile to strangers as the worthies represented in that charming sketch in *Punch* some years ago—

"It's a stranger, let's 'eave 'alf a brick at him;" yet there is everywhere the feeling, "It's a stranger, let's make what we can out of him."

The dialect, too, is fearfully Bavarian—ugly and broad. Of course the German we are taught in England by Hanoverians, is here considered—by the country people, at least—as singularly affected and contemptible! The townspeople and higher orders speak very easy and pretty German—far superior to the shrill Deutsch one hears in Vienna. The dialect of Brünn am Geberge is the worst I ever heard. Some of the words were perfectly unintelligible to me. When they told me not to walk that road, for there was a "hog" at the end, I had to reflect some minutes before I came to the conclusion that they might possibly mean a "Hecke," or hedge. I have often been startled by some warning about a *Thier* (beast), till I discovered that the "beast" in question was a *Thür* (door). In other parts of Germany, we are accustomed to have cream offered to us with tea, as "Rahm," or "Sahne." One looks rather at a loss, therefore, when "Oberst" is proposed to him, perhaps in his first surprise thinking that, if he should give his assent, a colonel or some high official may be popped into his tea-cup.

Chapter XIV.

POST-OFFICE ROUTINE—STAMPS—OFFICIAL NEGLECT—PROGRESS OF AUSTRIA—MÖNCHBERG—CHATEAU OF AIGEN—THE GAISBERG—POLITENESS OF SOLDIERS—FOX-SHOOTING—PREPARATIONS FOR WINTER—COLD NIGHTS—THE PEASANTS AT HOME.

CHAPTER XIV.

THE most troublesome people we have come in contact with are decidedly those of the post-office. The wearisome routine, the unnecessary formalities, of this Royal institution try one's temper sadly. If one sends a parcel by post, he must seal it with a fabulous number of seals—fourteen is no unusual number. Before a parcel can be sent by post to England, five papers must be signed. The transmission of a registered letter is almost as formidable an affair as making a last will and testament!

I was intensely amused one day when I took a small wooden box to the post-office in Salzburg, to send by post. It contained only a small stag's head, carved in wood, which I wished copied, and was to go no further than Ebensee. It was solemnly received by an official, who leisurely read the direction, and with official dignity turned the box over. It was then handed to another, who, after inspecting it as cautiously and minutely as if it had been an infernal machine, consulted a third. When a rather lengthened consultation was ended, they informed me that they regretted they could not send it, as there were no seals to it. I said I had no sealing-wax, and that as it was so light, I thought it would go perfectly well without. Such a thing, they said, was not to be thought of. I cast an imploring look at a big stick of sealing-wax, nearly as thick as my wrist, which was lying on a desk; but that mute appeal to official benevolence remained unanswered. I supposed they considered it would be a wholesome lesson in Imperial routine if I had to take a little trouble.

With a look of silent indignation, which was entirely disregarded, I took up my little box, and went across with it from the post-office to the Schiff Hotel, where I begged the son of the landlady to procure for me the necessary materials. He very obligingly got light and wax, soon covered the box with a surprising number of seals, wrote out the direction on a half sheet of paper, and affixed a stamp of five kreutzers to it. Armed with this and my decorated box, I again approached the officials. Once more my box was handed from one to the other, and scrutinized as narrowly as if they had not seen it five minutes before. One faithful servant of the Emperor's suggested one more seal in a spot where, by great exertions, the string that was tied round the box might have been moved the tenth part of an inch! Luckily for my patience, and the credit of an Englishwoman for good manners, this objection was overruled; and after signing another paper, the Government undertook the important charge, and I got rid of my box.

Stamps are a great institution in Austria. They have to be bought for everything. When a bill is sent in it has a stamp. Every almanack has one. No one would depend on a servant's written character without one. Every newspaper we receive must have a receipt-stamp as well as the post-stamp on it. All the printed forms of law, and all military papers, have several. I used to expect to see a stamp on the bills of fare. In short, the routine of Imperial business seems a marvellous mixture of unnecessary punctilio, conjoined in many cases with an utter want of precaution, In fact, the system appears occasionally to overleap itself.

When an officer marries he has to lodge a sum of money in the hands of his considerate Kaiser, as a future provision for his widow or children. If he is under thirty the sum lodged is 24,000 Gulden. After thirty it is 12,000; and if on half-pay, 6,000. For this they are promised five per cent.; but officers having been lately included in the number of those who pay income-tax, they only get about three per cent. for it. If the State becomes bankrupt—which happened in the last Emperor's time—all the caution-money, as it is called, goes in the general ruin, and no one can imagine the misery that is entailed.

When the officer places this money in the hands of the official appointed to receive it, he has to leave it for some time without even obtaining a receipt for it. Last month a lieutenant had lodged his caution-money, and the next morning the agent absconded, carrying off the sum with him. The papers have been full of advertisements, the object of which is the discovery of "Edward Lachermaier, Military Register Official," and of the unfortunate officer's 6,000 florins.

One must not, however, expect too much at once; and notwithstanding the large army and the dread of bankruptcy, Austria is every day getting more busy and more satisfied. Useful reforms are carried out. The Government is laying the foundation of improved institutions. The nation is beginning to understand that active industry will be more effective in developing the resources of their rich and splendid country than the subjugation of unwilling races, the extension of their conquests, or reliance on the chimera of a feeble Bund.

Still, proper precautions are not neglected. Every day, from the citadel above us, we hear, at stated hours, the reserve corps practising with the new breech-loading guns. The drilled soldiers have already learned their exercise, and they are now calling up the reserve corps for practice. Lately an order has been issued that no soldiers are henceforward to be addressed in the second person singular, as heretofore, but in the second person plural, as more respectful to men who carry arms. The officers laugh, and shake their heads at this new regulation, and up to the present moment have not generally obeyed it, for I always hear them calling the soldiers, when off duty, by the old accustomed "Du." I suppose, by degrees, they will get reconciled to the change, as well as to the substitution of blue for white uniforms—but that they sadly regret the latter no one can doubt.

I cannot understand why Salzburg is not more known, more talked about, and more praised in England than it is. It certainly strikes me as not only one of the most beautifully-situated towns that I ever saw, but also as such an excellent place whence to make excursions. The town is very like

Edinburgh, only, instead of the well-arranged streets of the new town, those in Salzburg are narrow, old-fashioned ones. Instead of the Calton Hill, there is the beautiful Capucinenberg, with its wooded sides enclosed above the rocky base with a picturesque line of wall and towers. Instead of the one rock on which Edinburgh Castle stands, there is a much higher and more broken range of rocks, crowned on its highest summit by the old fortress, and in other parts covered with luxuriant beech woods and fertile meadows, among which, every here and there, a strong-looking powder-magazine, or a high watch-tower, reminds us that we are just on the verge of what has been an enemy's country.

The Mönchsberg is a strikingly beautiful place for those who can stand the keen air of Salzburg. Perhaps it is for this reason that it is not half appreciated by the inhabitants. The few houses are soon closed in autumn; and, in my many wanderings over it, I have met very few people. It is wonderful that it should be so, for after we have surmounted the many flights of steps, or the steep road that leads up to it from the town, how ample is the reward! Exquisite views meet us at every turn. Wandering on for hours, we may find fresh beauties to delight us. In the full blaze of sunlight, at sunset, and even by starlight, new views disclose themselves.

I have never yet managed to walk there at that early hour when, as the poetic German guide-books remarks, "Any one will be enchanted to observe the heavy mists roll from the mountains and sink in the valleys, and the white rocky mountain summits change from the pale pink of Silene to the full rich crimson of the 'Rose des Alpes;'" but at every other time the view has been so charming, that it requires very little imagination to form a vivid picture of the above description without having to undergo the ordeal of such early rising. The fields on the summit are beautiful in early spring, I am told, with the lovely wild-flowers which abound round Salzburg. Now they are only ornamented with the pale autumn crocus and the thickly-falling gold and scarlet leaves of the thorn and maples.

We took a sharp drive one day to the Château of Aigen, belonging to Prince Schwarzenberg. The house itself is nothing to look at, nor are the gardens round it. The most pleasant recollection is of some excellent coffee we drank under the shady trees, at a restaurant which the Prince has obligingly allowed to be established at his back-door! The walks beyond the gardens are through shady woods of fine forest-trees, by the side of small mountain streams, over neat rustic bridges, and up winding hill-sides, which are shaded and cool, and from which we have peeps, through the thick foliage, of distant mountain-tops clothed in dazzling snow.

One such view is not far from the house, and is well worth the drive from Salzburg on purpose to see it alone. In a frame of thick beech-boughs is a sunny picture of fields and moors stretching for miles towards the mountains, and crowned by the pointed and peaked summits of the Watzmann, which is certainly the most striking-looking of the chain of mountains that surround Salzburg, but which we cannot see from that city, as it is shut out by the grim Untersberg.

From Aigen the ascent of the Gaisberg is made, and the view obtained from the summit is considered well worth the climb; but we were too happy and contented with our easy wood walks to think of toil. It was nearly as warm as it is in June, and we were glad to rest at the before-mentioned restaurant, and drink some hot coffee, while others had good sparkling beer, served by a smart-looking man of unmistakeably soldier-like appearance. On inquiring if he had not been a soldier, his answer, with a beaming smile to our friend, was, "I served under you in Italy, my Colonel."

The soldiers are very much more sociable than in England. I suppose this may be owing to the pleasant ease and natural freedom of foreign manners. Those who had been to the house with messages, or who had ever spoken with any of the family, if we met them again, would always remove their cigars, and exchange some polite greeting as we passed.

The peasants, every holiday, employ their time in practising rifle-shooting at different villages, and they are mostly excellent marksmen, though they have not many opportunities of proving their skill, except at the bull's eye. Game, which is scarce round Salzburg, is strictly preserved. Two gentlemen dined with us one evening, on their return from a long shooting excursion, and, except a couple of wild deer, their bag boasted only of three foxes. One can never get used to the idea of a fox being shot as anything legitimate, and I shall never, I fear, learn to repress a strong inclination to laugh when I am informed of the result of a day's fox-shooting.

Small, different-coloured rosettes are given to the soldiers, to wear in their caps as rewards or decorations for skilful shooting. I have counted as many as nine in some of the men's caps. The nearer they hit the bull's eye, the larger is the rosette. The largest are about the size of half-a-crown, and the small ones are about the diameter of a sixpence. Some of the soldiers have the one side of their caps nearly covered with them.

My holiday is drawing to a close, and I must soon be thinking of returning to England. Already the swallows, which here build in the most sociable way inside front halls and over kitchen doors, have taken their departure to the sunny south. It is becoming in the early mornings so cold, that the maid-servants talk confidentially of leaving off starch in their own and the children's cotton-dresses—a precaution always adopted here in winter! In England we generally trust to our luck that it may be a mild winter, and the preparations we make are very small in fortifying ourselves and our houses against cold. But here it is perfectly formidable to see the work that is going on. The plants that have adorned the terraces and verandahs of Salzburg during the bright summer days are already safely housed. Double windows are snugly fitted in; the weather-side of verandahs are tightly boarded over; the beautiful public fountains in the town are being fast converted into large wooden erections. Every statue, every carved gravestone, every sun-dial, is being swathed in straw. Even the rose-trees and stocks are enveloped in great-coats; and everywhere the town looks as if preparing for a siege.

Passing lately by a house on our ledge of rock, I found that all the tall vines that had decorated it so luxuriantly up to the third story, had been stripped down, and were now being pruned, doubled up, and packed away in the most uncomfortable-looking manner, under a boarding of wood. I stopped and begged to know the reason. They told me it was always done in winter, for that, if left growing against the houses, they would not survive the cold. Next week, they informed me, the vines against the Colonel's house would be served in the same manner.

I have a great wish to see Salzburg in its winter dress. I am told that, when everything here has been covered with a week's steady snowing, the frost is so keen, and there is such a remarkable absence of wind, that the snow lies in wreaths upon the trees and fences, and in piles of such depth upon the ground as are seldom seen elsewhere. Everything about, however, is still in such full autumn luxuriance, the foliage is so abundant, and the colours so beautiful, that I feel I should be sorry to watch the gradual decay of all this beauty. I should regret to see the luxuriant vines, from which I had picked in the hot sunshine such delicious bunches of grapes, all laid down in the dust, and their dead leaves swept unceremoniously away.

It has rained heavily the last few days, and though the red umbrellas of the peasants, glancing in and out through the yellow, green, and scarlet foliage, in the plains below, make the landscape look almost cheerful, yet the chains of mountains beyond are already clad in their white winter robes. Untersberg no longer stands out in that hard, iron-grey hue which is natural to it, but its rugged peaks, its pine forests, and even the deserted huts of the herdsmen, are covered with a smooth mantle of spotless snow, which rounds and softens them.

It is freezingly cold in the nights, and the winter stoves are so invitingly warm, that the peasants have no inclination to wander out in the cold moonlight that glimmers so drearily over Untersberg's wintry shroud, to discover whether, under the frosty starlight of winter, as in the warm summer nights, the gnomes pace wearily over the mountain, looking longingly and eagerly for the first welcome

U

signs of release. Alas! alas! for the hope of a united Fatherland! It has long been gradually dying away from living breasts, and soon the only spot in Germany round which the vain legend will cling will be the Kaiser's grave in mighty Untersberg.

Chapter XV.

L'HOMME PROPOSE, DIEU DISPOSE—SALZBURG UNDER ITS WINTER ASPECT—UNEXPECTED DEATH OF A KIND FRIEND—END OF THE SOLDIER'S WARFARE—GOD'S-ACRE—FUNERAL OF LIEUTENANT-COLONEL RITTER VON ARI.

CHAPTER XV.

WE went cheerfully on through the bright autumn months, enjoying the present, and planning Alpine excursions and long mountain expeditions for next year. All that we were too idle, or too contented with our home happiness, to accomplish now, we intended to crowd into next summer. Alas! for us short-sighted mortals—my wish to see Salzburg in snow, winter, and tempest was too speedily gratified, but in a very different way from that which we had hoped and planned.

I had left Salzburg in the last days of October, bright and sunny, all decked in its golden autumnal colouring. A fortnight passed, and I was again there, in the beautiful Salzkammergut, in the pretty house at Nonnberg, that nestles under the rocks and citadel, in the home which I had left so recently in all its cheerful brightness; but how changed in those few days! Not only had the heavy autumn winds and the wintry tempests shaken ruthlessly every golden vestige of bright summer from the trees, but the white snow was spread over the wide plains and distant mountains, far as the eye could see. Hanging in thick masses, it weighed down every tiny twig and stem. It had swept into the recesses of the vast pine forests. Every little frozen rill and stream was covered with it.

But blank and dreary as was the aspect of nature, it was not half so desolate as that home where we had passed so many bright days. In our short absence, the Angel of Death had visited it, and the heart of the survivor refused to be comforted. With the first sharp days of winter, the worshipped husband, the loving father, and the warm-hearted friend had been suddenly summoned away. The brave soldier's warfare was accomplished, and all his toils and troubles were over for ever!

Once more I gazed from the windows where I had so often stood with him, joining in his admiration of those beautiful changes of colour which in this marvellously lovely view come over the clouds and mountains. A thick fog now rolled heavily over everything, enveloping at once mountains and plains. It was so dense that we could not catch a glimpse even of the blue sky, beyond which we hoped our departed friend now was. Instead of his cheerful voice, I could only in fancy hear, amid the wailing music of the death march, the heavy tread of the soldiers as they bore him to his honoured grave.

Once more I stood under the Capucinenberg, while the setting sun gleamed on its summit with a sickly light. I was in a quiet burying-ground (or "God's-acre," as they call it in Germany), where I was about to hang a wreath of glossy bay-leaves and pure white chrysanthemum blossoms—picked in a far-away English garden—over the grave of one who, only a fortnight before, had said to me in the parting salutation of his country, "Come back again soon." And here I was back again, but not as we intended. He who does all things well, without whose permission not even a sparrow falls to the ground, had ordained it otherwise. Here I was, "back again," my frail life mercifully preserved in those two short weeks through storms by sea and land, and the fearful peril of a railway collision, and he, the seemingly strong man, who had spoken those words, had by his own hearth succumbed to a mortal disease. But it was in His good time, though to us it seemed all too soon.

In that quiet, pretty churchyard, those English flowers hang side by side, with wreaths of immortelles and Edelweis, and with a crown of faded laurel leaves, which the loving hands of mourning relatives and comrades had already placed there. Masses are said and prayers are breathed daily and hourly for the repose of that soul which *we* trust is safely landed in the haven of eternal rest.

I cannot close this chapter without showing how highly loved and esteemed my lost friend was, by giving the account of his funeral from the papers.

"The last sad rites were paid to the late lamented Lieut.-Colonel Prinzinger von Ari on Thursday last. The melancholly procession formed at four o'clock at his late residence in the Nonnberg. The coffin was borne on the shoulders of sixteen soldiers, and twenty-four others followed, carrying lighted flambeaux. Then came the members of the family as chief mourners.

"As the mournful train was leaving the house a salute was fired by the soldiers. Arrived at the foot of the Nonnberg, the whole garrison formed in order and joined, most of the officers being devoted friends and comrades of the deceased. By command of the Archduke Charles (the father of the Emperor of Austria) the procession, headed by the fine military band, playing a funeral march, passed through the court of the Imperial residence, and from thence by the principal streets to the burying-place at St. Sebastian.

"Arrived at the grave of his parents, the solemn service was read, the soldiers fired three volleys, and the mournful rite was over.

"The deceased officer, Adolf Prinzinger Ritter von Ari, was until lately Lieut.-Colonel of the 14th Infantry Regiment (Grossherzog von Hesse), in the Austrian army. He served under Radetzky in 1848, again in Italy in 1859, and through the campaign in 1866. For his services and bravery he was decorated with the Iron Crown, the military service cross and crown, the order of Louis of Hesse, and the Grand Duke Charles Frederick of Baden's military service order.

"Many were the tears wept over his grave, not only by his brave companions in arms, but also by the residents and principal inhabitants of Salzburg, who had joined the funeral train, anxious to show this last token of respect to the dead. Every one who knew him honoured and loved him, and all his comrades and friends lamented together that Austria had lost one of her bravest and most devoted soldiers!"

THE END.

www.ingramcontent.com/pod-product-compliance
Lightning Source LLC
Chambersburg PA
CBHW022103230426
43672CB00008B/1268